THE SACRED HEART FOR LENT

THE SACRED HEART FOR LENT

DAILY MEDITATIONS

THOMAS D. WILLIAMS

PUBLISHED BY ST. ANTHONY MESSENGER PRESS
CINCINNATI, OHIO

Cover and book design by Mark Sullivan
Cover image © Shutterstock | Zvonimir Atletic

LIBRARY OF CONGRESS CATALOGING-IN-PUBLICATION DATA
Williams, Thomas D., LC.
The sacred heart for Lent : daily meditations / Thomas D. Williams.
p. cm.
Includes bibliographical references and index.
ISBN 978-1-61636-238-6 (pbk. : alk. paper) 1. Lent—Prayers and devotions. 2. Lent—Meditations. I. Title.
BV85.W468 2011
242'.34—dc23
2011038865

ISBN: 978-1-61636-238-6

Published by Servant Books, an imprint of St. Anthony Messenger Press.
28 W. Liberty St.
Cincinnati, OH 45202
www.AmericanCatholic.org
www.ServantBooks.org

Printed in the United States of America

Printed on acid-free paper

11 12 13 14 15   5 4 3 2 1

To celebrate the Heart of Christ means to turn toward the profound center of the Person of the Savior, that center which the Bible identifies precisely as his Heart, seat of the love that has redeemed the world. If the human heart represents an unfathomable mystery that only God knows, how much more sublime is the heart of Jesus, in which the life of the Word itself beats. In it…are found all the treasures of wisdom and science and all the fullness of divinity.

—*Blessed John Paul II, address before the Angelus,*
St. Peter's Square, June 24, 2002

Contents

Introduction

Lent is the ideal time of the year to get to know Jesus better. In this blessed period, our hearts are disposed to pray more, to deny ourselves, and to serve others. Among the different devotions that help us draw nearer to Christ, few are as fruitful as devotion to his Sacred Heart.

Pope Pius XI wrote in his encyclical letter *Miserentissimus Redemptor,* "Is not a summary of all our religion and, moreover, a guide to a more perfect life contained in this one devotion [to the Sacred Heart]? Indeed, it more easily leads our minds to know Christ the Lord intimately and more effectively turns our hearts to love him more ardently and to imitate him more perfectly."[1] That is the whole point of this little book. The simple meditations I offer in this volume are meant to deepen the journey of Christians through Lent by helping them to learn how to know Christ more intimately, love him more profoundly, and imitate him more perfectly.

Traditionally, devotion to the Sacred Heart of Jesus has consisted especially in two aspects: *expiation* and *imitation.* Jesus reveals to us his heart that has so loved humanity and yet receives in return so little love and so little gratitude. We *expiate* this ingratitude and indifference when we try to love Jesus more, to give him a bigger place in our hearts and lives, and when we learn to appreciate more fully his infinite love for us. What better time than Lent to seek to console the heart of Christ? In the Garden of Gethsemane, Jesus experienced profound loneliness and begged his apostles to accompany him, to stay awake with him. He did not want to be alone. This Lent, we have the opportunity to respond to that plea. We will not leave him alone.

Along with expiation, devotion to the Sacred Heart also means *imitation*. As we get to know Jesus more personally and intimately, we are drawn to want to be like him. His personality is attractive and fascinating—huge crowds followed him around Palestine, hanging on his every word and happy just to be close to him. Everyone wanted to be with him: little children, the elderly, simple people, sinners, educated leaders. In the heart of Christ we discover our ideal: what human beings were meant to be. He reveals to us how good humanity can be, how good you and I could be! As we contemplate the many facets of the heart of Jesus, his virtues and qualities, we find a blueprint for our own lives. Each of us was created to become like Jesus.

If we want to know who *we* are, who we were created to be, we will find the answer in Jesus Christ and especially in his *heart*. This Lent, my prayer is that our contemplation of Jesus Christ and his heart will reveal God to us and reveal our true selves as well.

Lord, let me know you so well that I cannot help but love you. Let me love you so deeply that I cannot help but want to be like you. As I spend this Lent with you, make my heart more like yours!

1. Pius XI, *Miserrentissimus Redemptor* (1928), 3, as quoted by Pius XII in the English translation of *Haurietis Aquas* (1956), 15.

Lent Begins

How blessed we Christians are to have this season of forty days to prepare for Holy Week and Easter! The most important and solemn event of the liturgical year is coming, and the Church offers us this grace-filled time to get ready for it. Most of this preparation is internal, rather than external. We endeavor to get our hearts ready to contemplate the mysteries of Jesus' passion, death, and resurrection. We strive to tune in to what the Holy Spirit is doing in our lives, to purify ourselves of those things that prevent us from being the people that God wants us to be, and to give ourselves generously to our brothers and sisters. Let's commit ourselves to taking advantage of this precious season like never before!

Ash Wednesday

Beware of practicing your piety before men in order to
be seen by them; for then you will have no reward from
your Father who is in heaven. Thus, when you give alms,
sound no trumpet before you, as the hypocrites do in the
synagogues and in the streets, that they may be praised by
men. Truly, I say to you, they have their reward. But when
you give alms, do not let your left hand know what your
right hand is doing, so that your alms may be in secret;
and your Father who sees in secret will reward you.

Matthew 6:1–4

Jesus recognized that we often do the right thing for the wrong reason.
For instance, we sometimes pray publicly in order to be thought of
as holy or pious. Sometimes people give generous donations in order
to be praised or thought of highly. Sure, we do things for God, but a
little human recognition strokes our ego and makes us feel good about
ourselves. Jesus unmasks these practices, because he doesn't want our
twisted intentions to deprive us of the rewards he has in store for us. His
new law is all about having both our inside and our outside in line with
God's will. In his own words, he doesn't just want us "good," he wants
us perfect!

Jesus himself gives the supreme example of this. He really didn't care
much what people thought of him. He didn't care whether they praised
him or censured him. He wasn't looking for human approval at all and
had no interest in being popular. It wasn't that Jesus didn't care about
other people, but their judgment of him didn't carry much weight—he
was much more concerned with what God thought of him. And so

Jesus was free to say what needed to be said and to do what needed to be done. He didn't trample other people's feelings, but he didn't allow human respect to keep him from doing the right thing either. With Jesus, what you saw is what you got. He was the same on the inside and the outside.

Lord, what a beautiful example you give me! Help me to love you more and to strive to please you alone. If I realize that I am always in your presence and that your opinion is the only one that really counts, it will be easier for me to act with purity of intention. Let me love others but not care so much about their opinions of me. I know I can't please everyone, and the one I ultimately want to please is you!

Sacred Heart of Jesus, unpretentious and pure of intent, make my heart more like yours!

THURSDAY AFTER ASH WEDNESDAY

If any man would come after me, let him deny himself
and take up his cross daily and follow me. For whoever
would save his life will lose it; and whoever loses his life
for my sake, he will save it. For what does it profit a man
if he gains the whole world and loses or forfeits himself?

—*Luke 9:23–25*

. . .

Oddly, in many ways Jesus reveals a businessman's personality. He often reasoned in terms of costs and benefits, of investments and yield. He expected his disciples to bear fruit, and he looked for a return on the talents he bestowed. He was not some wild-eyed idealist but a firmly grounded realist. At the same time, Jesus' style of realism was eternity-based and not earthly. Short-term gains didn't impress him, since his goal for each of us is eternal life. And so he encouraged his followers to discover the true value of things and to pursue what counted in the long run.

This realism is expressed in today's verses from Luke. Note that Jesus doesn't tell us not to look for profit but rather to look for *real* profit, profit that matters. He invites us to be reasonable, to consider which investments are really worth the trouble and which ones aren't. Jesus lived according to this code. He didn't waste time with investments that weren't going to yield a profit that's eternal. Every moment of his life was spent in pursuits that were more fruitful, with an eye on the ultimate bottom line: the salvation of souls. Jesus knew what was important, and he never deviated from his course. Lent is our chance to reorder our own values and priorities so that they coincide with God's.

Lord, you saw things clearly. You kept your priorities straight, even when tempted by tantalizing offers or threatened with horrible punishments. Thank you for your example of clarity and good business sense. This lenten season, help me value heaven more than anything I can acquire on earth. Remind me often that everything here is passing and that only heaven lasts forever.

Sacred Heart of Jesus, realistic and eternal in your pursuits, make my heart more like yours!

Friday after Ash Wednesday

The Pharisees…said to his disciples, "Why does your
teacher eat with tax collectors and sinners?" But when
[Jesus] heard it, he said, "Those who are well have no
need of a physician, but those who are sick. Go and
learn what this means, 'I desire mercy, and not sacrifice.' For I came not to call the righteous, but sinners."
—*Matthew 9:10–13*

. . .

The heart of Jesus is a heart rich in mercy, a heart that is moved with
pity in the face of human misery, especially the moral misery of sin.
Jesus is not an uninterested judge, dispensing rewards and punishments
with the same indifference. Like the Father, Jesus desires not the death
of the sinner but rather that he turn from his evil ways and live (cf.
Ezekiel 18:23). He defends his constant company-keeping with sinners
by reminding his hearers that he's a physician who has come not for the
healthy but for the sick (cf. Matthew 9:11–13). His entire mission, in
fact, is a mission of mercy. Pope John Paul, in his encyclical letter *Dives
in Misericordia,* did not hesitate to say that Jesus' words "Blessed are the
merciful" constitute a "synthesis of the whole of the Good News."[1] The
gospel is, above all, a message of the mercy of God.

In a real sense, when we are merciful we touch the most distinctive
quality of Christ's own heart. We resemble him in the most intimate
way possible. As Pope John Paul wrote, during the time of our earthly
existence "love must be revealed above all as mercy and must also be
actualized as mercy."[2] If we want to know whether we love like Christ,
we must ask ourselves whether our heart is merciful as his was. Without

mercy, love is impossible. While justice is indeed necessary, it is insufficient by itself. Just as we wouldn't want God to apply strict justice in judging us, we must be ready to forgive our neighbor.

Lord, where would I be without your infinite mercy? How many times have I turned to you in sorrow only to hear those saving words, "My child, I forgive you"? Let me always have your mercy before my eyes, so that I will not be tempted to desire for others a punishment that I have been spared. Help me to detest sin and do what I can to eradicate it, above all in my own life. At the same time, let me look on my fellow sinners with a heart of mercy, with your own heart. If I am to err, Lord, let it be on the side of mercy!

Heart of Jesus, full of merciful love,
make my heart more like yours!

1. John Paul II, *Dives in Misericordia* (2008), 8.
2. *Dives in Misericordia*, 8.

SATURDAY AFTER ASH WEDNESDAY

Then Jesus was led up by the Spirit into the wilderness to
be tempted by the devil. And he fasted forty days and forty
nights, and afterward he was hungry. And the tempter came
and said to him, "If you are the Son of God, command
these stones to become loaves of bread." But he answered,
"It is written, 'Man shall not live by bread alone, but by
every word that proceeds from the mouth of God.'"

—*Matthew 4:1–4*

. . .

Nobody likes to be tested. It's not fun to have to engage in spiritual war-
fare and fight against inclinations and options that we know are wrong
but that exert pressure on us anyway. We would like "doing good" to
be easy. Yet Jesus gives us a supreme example of how to deal with temptation. He doesn't entertain it. He doesn't consider sin an option. He
knows that the only path for him is the one that the Father has marked
out for him.

How blessed we are to have a Savior who was tempted in every way
we are yet never sinned (cf. Hebrews 4:15). As our Good Shepherd he
walks before us, showing us how to confront the devil and his tempta-
tions and how to triumph. He reminds us that bread alone and all that
it represents (material and temporal goods) is necessary but radically
insufficient. The world's deepest problems—and ours as well—cannot
be resolved with more money, more houses, more food, more "things."
Only God truly satisfies the human heart. Only his word fills us and
leaves us fully content and satiated.

Lord, you knew what it was to want. You felt hunger and thirst. You naturally preferred comfort to discomfort and pleasure to pain, and yet this was never your primary concern. For you, the one thing that truly mattered was doing the will of your Heavenly Father. Help me to acquire your criteria, your moral clarity, your courage in standing up to temptation. Above all, let me never waver in my commitment to God and his will as my one, true good.

Sacred Heart of Jesus, hungry for God,
make my heart more like yours!

Week One

As we begin the first week of Lent, we look to get into a good rhythm of spiritual work—carving time out of each day for conversation with the Lord, paying special attention to the needs of those around us, and offering little sacrifices that keep us focused on the one thing necessary (cf. Luke 10:42).

Lord Jesus, I have proposed to spend this Lent together with you. That's what I desire more than anything. I want to be more and more yours and to experience the intense love that you have for me. Grant me this grace, I beg you. Let me rediscover you this week as the one thing that truly matters. I love you and want to love you more and more. Amen.

SUNDAY—WEEK ONE

Come to me, all you who are weary and are burdened, and I will give you rest. Take my yoke upon
you and learn from me, for I am meek and humble
of heart; and you will find rest for yourselves.
—*Matthew 11:28–29,* NAB

. . .

There is no more "classic" virtue of the heart of Christ than his humility.
He invites us to *learn* from him and tells us that he is *meek* and *humble*
of heart. Jesus then goes on to promise rest and refreshment for our
souls, and who doesn't need that? But what does it mean to "shoulder
his yoke" and learn to be "meek and humble"? What about those of us
with strong, "alpha" temperaments?

To say that Jesus was "meek and humble" certainly doesn't mean he
was a wimp. The strength of his character was unsurpassed. He was a
true leader, with clear ideals, deep convictions, and an iron will. Yet at
the same time he had time for the "little people"—beggars, poor people,
children, prostitutes, tax men. He never acted superior to the people he
was with but listened to their problems and came to their assistance. He
knew that he was "Lord," and yet he never "lorded" it over anyone.

So what about us? Humility is a funny virtue, because we love it in
others but have a hard time practicing it ourselves. We like to be appre-
ciated. We like to be right. We often compare ourselves to others (sometimes feeling superior, other times envious, still other times bitterly infe-
rior). If we are honest, we find in ourselves a lot of pride that we don't
see in Jesus. Yet Jesus promises that the yoke of humility is sweet. When
we shoulder it and let go of ourselves, we find "rest for our souls"!

Lord, help me to love humility. Let me not fear humiliations, because you love me and that should be enough. All I have is what you have given me, so what is there for me to be vain about? Instead, let me be grateful for my gifts and put them all at the disposal of others and your kingdom. Let people find in me—as they found in you—a humble heart, a welcoming smile, and a listening ear.

**Sacred Heart of Jesus, meek and humble,
make my heart more like yours!**

MONDAY—WEEK ONE

I was thirsty and you gave me drink.... Truly, I say to you,
as you did it to one of these my brethren, you did it to me.
—*Matthew 25:35, 40*

. . .

Jesus says that whenever someone gives drink to a thirsty person, he considers it done to him. But he also expresses his own thirst, both on the cross (cf. John 19:28) and in his encounter with the Samaritan woman at Jacob's well (cf. John 4:4–42). What could be more poignant than our suffering Lord, who appeals to us from his Passion: "I thirst!"

Jesus thirsts, all right, but he doesn't thirst just for water. His heart thirsts for souls. He thirsts for love. This thirst isn't some narcissistic need to be loved; Jesus craves our love because he wants to fill us with himself. He wants to give us a joy that we can know only by loving him. Jesus' thirst for love is a thirst *to give love.* That's why, when he meets the Samaritan woman at the well, his request for a drink quickly transforms into a promise of living water (cf. John 4:14).

We too can thirst for the salvation of souls. And we can also quench Christ's thirst. Much of the traditional devotion to the Sacred Heart focused on consoling the heart of Christ, making reparation for sins. This is a very practical way to ease the very real thirst of Christ's heart. This Lent, we can look for opportunities to teach souls about his love, bring them closer to him through our prayer and good example, and draw closer ourselves to his heart, knowing that all these things console him. We can also pray in a special way for those people we know who are far from him and whose return to his side would truly satisfy his thirst.

Lord, when I see you on the cross, I want to find a way to alleviate your thirst. I know that it wasn't just water you were longing for—you thirst for the love of all those you came to save. Let me find some way today to slake your thirst. Send your Holy Spirit to inspire me so that I will spot real opportunities to show my love for you and console your heart, maybe by some small sacrifice to prove my preference to you above all things, or maybe by an act of kindness to someone in need.

**Sacred Heart of Jesus, thirsty for souls,
make my heart more like yours!**

TUESDAY—WEEK ONE

If you forgive others their failings, your heavenly Father
will forgive you yours; but if you do not forgive others,
your Father will not forgive your failings either.

—*Matthew 6:15*, JB

. . .

Why is it that we do not feel for sinners the same pity that Jesus felt?
Why are we moved with pity at the suffering of a beaver with its leg
caught in a trap and yet for sinners feel nothing but anger and disdain?
Perhaps we feel that they had a choice, that it is their own fault. Choices
have consequences, and they chose badly. Yet when we reason in this
way, we separate ourselves radically from the heart of Christ. The world
reveres justice as the greatest virtue, but forgiveness distinguishes the
Christian.

The heart of Jesus thirsts for souls. He truly loves sinners and longs
for their conversion. He rejoices when they return to him. When Jesus
sees a sinner, he feels not anger or repugnance but the deepest compassion, up to the point of being willing to shed his blood for that person.
He desires not their death, or their eternal condemnation, but their
redemption and eternal joy.

Sinners can be a big turn-off for Christians. We feel uncomfortable in
their presence. We don't want to be contaminated by their filth, much
as health workers may avoid too much contact with an infectious dis-
ease. Thank God we aren't like them, we think. Thank God we've been
saved from all that! Yet we are called to love them, to suffer for them,
to ardently desire their good. In the end, we are all in the same boat, all
desperately in need of God's merciful love and the redemption that Jesus
brings. This Lent, let us remember that Jesus sought out the company

of sinners, not to engage in their ways but to extend the gift of mercy. When we do the same, we console his Heart.

Lord, this Lent help me realize that the world isn't divided into "us" and "them," the sinners and the saints. Let me feel the same compassion and love for sinners that you feel, and let me see that I too am a sinner in need of your grace and mercy. Teach me to love not only healthy, beautiful souls but those that are difficult to love, for, in loving them, I am loving you.

**Sacred Heart of Jesus, doctor of sinful souls,
make my heart more like yours!**

WEDNESDAY—WEEK ONE

You shall love the Lord your God with all your heart,
and with all your soul, and with all your mind.

—Matthew 22:37

. . .

• •

If anyone in history had an undivided heart, it was Jesus. He was totally committed to his Father and allowed no rivals to stain this undivided love. There is no wavering, no hemming and hawing, no second-guessing. Jesus had no secret vices, no attachments, no crutches he couldn't live without. He made his choice and stuck with it. He was happily committed and thoroughly faithful.

Jesus watched over his heart and made sure that nothing unworthy could ever take his Father's place. He used things, he loved people, but he worshipped his Father alone. For this reason, the Father's will was his supreme rule of conduct. In all things, he wanted to please his Father, and he let nothing else usurp God's place. He invites us to be just as single-hearted in following him.

I think we can only imagine what it means to truly love God with *all* our heart...with this degree of purity and single-heartedness. Many things are so "important" for us that we easily put them on a scale, opposite of God's will, to see which is heavier! Even when we succeed in making God our supreme value, we still feel that he's in competition with many other loves and many other goals. Lent is a time of purification. We ask God to purify our love as gold and silver are purified, cleansed of all their impurities.

Lord Jesus, my heart is filled with many loves. Many of them are good and pure; others are disordered and in need of cleansing. I don't think I really love God "with all my heart," the way you love the Father, but I want to. I don't want a divided heart, Lord. I don't want you to compete with other gods in my life. You and only you deserve all my love. You alone are my Lord and my Savior, fully worthy of all my love and devotion. Let it be so!

Sacred Heart of Jesus, undivided and fully devoted, make my heart more like yours!

THURSDAY—WEEK ONE

Father, I thank you for hearing me. I
know that you always hear me.
—*John 11:41–42*, NAB

. . .

• •

By his words and example, Jesus teaches us a lot about God, but he also teaches us what it means to be really human. And one thing we know for sure is that as a man Jesus trusted God. Totally. Completely. Unconditionally. Even when he didn't see things perfectly clearly, or didn't understand why God was asking something of him, or didn't feel God's presence, he trusted him anyway. On the cross Jesus *felt* the absence, the utter abandonment of God (see Matthew 27:46), and yet he knows the Father loves him, and confidently prays: "Father, into your hands, I commit my spirit" (Luke 23:46).

We get a brief glimpse of this when Jesus' dear friend Lazarus dies. Before he raises Lazarus from the dead, Jesus prays aloud the words quoted above. He doesn't say that he *hopes* God hears him or that he *thinks* that God *probably* hears him. He says, "I *know* that you always hear me." This is absolute confidence.

This absolute trust wasn't something that Christ intended just for himself because of the special Father–Son relationship he had with God. He intended it for us as well. He assures his disciples that God cares for all his creation, even the birds of the air and the lilies of the field (cf. Matthew 6:26–30). Jesus said that even little sparrows are never forgotten in God's sight and that we are worth far more than they are to God (cf. Luke 12:6–7). All of this is to help us have the same trust in God that he had. He tells us to stop worrying and start trusting. Seek first his kingdom, and everything else will fall into place.

Lord Jesus, I need a heart more like yours, a heart so confident that I can wake up in the morning and go about my activities with the assurance that you are with me every step of the way: supporting me, encouraging me, strengthening me, attentive to my every need. I too know that you always hear me. I know that you share my sorrows and my joys. I know that you answer all my prayers, even when I don't immediately get what I want or expect. Make my trust grow!

**Sacred Heart of Jesus, confident and full of trust,
make my heart more like yours!**

FRIDAY—WEEK ONE

Where your treasure is, there will your heart be also.
—*Luke 12:34*

. . .

. . . .

Jesus was truly the opposite of a "man of the world." He was a man of heaven, a man who saw everything supernaturally, a man for whom only eternal truths were really interesting. He cared nothing for gossip, politics, who was in power, or the social affairs of his time. He didn't get excited about sports teams or economic markets or movements of the Roman troops. He cared about *people* and especially about *their relationship to God.* He cared about big questions, transcendent questions, spiritual questions. His thoughts tended upward, not downward. Earthly realities reminded him of heavenly realities.

We, on the other hand, experience the battle between being interested in worldly things and living by the spirit, which the apostle Paul so aptly describes in Romans 8. It is often easier to get excited about frivolities than about things that really matter. The spiritual life seems to require more work than does planning parties or community events. At prayer we may sometimes get distracted thinking about a party, but at a party we rarely get distracted thinking about prayer—unlike Jesus, who was decidedly a man of the spirit. He saw things in a spiritual way, evaluated things from a spiritual perspective, and related things to deeper, spiritual truths.

What a wonderful example you give me, Jesus, of what it means to live as a spiritual person! Your priorities were always clear, and you always placed eternal truths above earthly concerns. All of creation became a window to your Father. Thank you for being for me a model of how to think and act with a heavenly heart.

**Sacred Heart of Jesus, focused on heaven,
make my heart more like yours!**

Saturday—Week One

Love your enemies and pray for those who persecute
you, so that you may be sons of your Father who is in
heaven; for he makes his sun rise on the evil and on the
good, and sends rain on the just and on the unjust.

—*Matthew 5:44–45*

. . .

• •

The universality of Christ's heart went to the extreme of loving even those who hated him and wished him ill. He never repaid evil but always responded with good. Most of us grew up hearing that Christians were supposed to love their enemies, so we can forget how genuinely novel and groundbreaking this teaching and behavior was.

Imagine what it was like for Jesus to travel, and eat, and joke around every day with Judas Iscariot, who, he knew, would betray him for thirty pieces of silver. He treated Judas with the same kindness, the same respect, and the same friendship that he showed the other apostles. He honored him by appointing him treasurer of the group, a position of trust. At the Last Supper, he even washes his feet.

So when Jesus tells his disciples, "Love your enemies," he knows full well what he is asking of them. He has felt in his own flesh how hard this is, and he knows what it means to will only good to the very one who is seeking with all his might to harm you.

Anytime we have been cheated or betrayed, anytime a friend, spouse, brother, or sister has let us down, anytime we have been judged harshly or spoken to unkindly, we have the opportunity to love our enemies. It is precisely when another person least deserves our love that we are directed to give it. In this way, we imitate the abundance and gratuitousness of God's love.

Lord Jesus, your example of magnanimity astounds and moves me. You never set limits on your love. You never asked, "Isn't that enough?" or "Hey, that's not fair!" You were willing to do anything, give anything, and suffer anything to save us. Help me to forget the wrongs done to me and to love my "enemies" as you loved yours. Let me begin by willing good for them, especially the greatest good: their salvation.

**Sacred Heart of Jesus, magnanimous in love,
make my heart more like yours!**

Week Two

In this second week of Lent we will contemplate Jesus' heart as it is passionately in love with his Father and with each of us. We will see how he kept it uncluttered and undivided so that nothing might distract him from his mission. Our first task is to contemplate the heart of Christ, to gaze on him and discover a love that knows no equal. This grateful contemplation will draw us to unbounded confidence in him, and to imitation.

Dear Jesus, I love getting to know you! There are always new facets of your personality to discover, always new virtues of your heart to contemplate. Draw me nearer and nearer to yourself. Reveal your Heart to me as you never have before. I want to feel the attractiveness of your Spirit; I ache to belong totally to you. Amen.

SUNDAY—WEEK TWO

In the temple [Jesus] found those who were selling oxen and
sheep and pigeons, and the money-changers at their business.
And making a whip of cords, he drove them all…out of the
temple; and he poured out the coins of the money-changers
and overturned their tables. And he told those who sold the
pigeons, "Take these things away; you shall not make my
Father's house a house of trade." His disciples remembered
that it was written, "Zeal for your house will consume me."

—*John 2:14–17*

. . .

Some paintings of Jesus make him look so dreamy-eyed and rosy-
cheeked that he comes across more like a 1960s flower child than a
crucified messiah. But these paintings don't do justice to the real Jesus.
Reading through the gospel accounts, we meet a Jesus with a much
richer personality, with great depth, sensitivity, wisdom, and passion.

Remember that the same Jesus who encouraged us to be innocent as
doves also invited us to be clever as serpents (cf. Matthew 10:16). The
same Jesus who said "Blessed are the meek" (Matthew 5:5) also coldly
censured the Pharisees, calling them a "brood of vipers" (Matthew
12:34). The same Jesus who embraced little children and cured lepers
also flipped over the tables in the temple, making a whip out of cords
and driving out the animals and money changers. It was this last scene
that made Jesus' disciples apply to him the scriptural verse (from Psalms
69:9) "Zeal for your house will consume me."

Jesus was zealous about the salvation of souls. He was zealous about
the Father's glory. He was the opposite of the apathetic, dispassionate,
androgynous image we sometimes see on holy cards. Jesus was on fire

with love for his Father and for souls, and this fire inflamed all his undertakings. Jesus had spiritual *drive*.

This doesn't mean that Christians should be running around like a
bunch of crazed fanatics, jumping up on soapboxes and screaming about
the end of the world. Not much is accomplished for Christ's kingdom
by acting like religious lunatics. Jesus was zealous—but he united his
zeal to prudence, ordering his behavior according to the Father's will.
His zeal expressed itself in many different ways, but it was always motivated by the same love and passion underneath.

*Lord, as I draw near to your Sacred Heart, let me be ignited with the fire
of your love. Shake me out of my apathy and laziness so that I can be a true
apostle of your kingdom. Let me burn with your fire, love with your love,
and feel toward all those around me the zeal you feel!*

**Sacred Heart of Jesus, full of zeal for the kingdom,
make my heart more like yours!**

MONDAY—WEEK TWO

As the Father has loved me, so have I
loved you; abide in my love.

—*John 15:9*

. . .

∙ ∙

The image of Jesus' heart revealed to St. Margaret Mary Alocoque was surrounded by flames, literally burning with love for us. Something impossible for us to fathom is the depth of Jesus' ardent love for souls. He doesn't just *put up* with us. He doesn't just *like* us. His heart is *on fire* with love for us. Think about the time you were most in love, multiply it by infinity, and you get a sense of how Jesus feels about us. And "us" here doesn't mean the mass of humanity. It means YOU. Jesus is literally dying for you to be in heaven with him. Each of us occupies the heart of Jesus in a unique, singular way.

We are called to be passionate like Christ. Our hearts should burn with love for God, for Jesus, for Mary, for the Church, and for our brothers and sisters. Christianity is not a religion of platonic goodwill toward all. It does not hold up "niceness" as the supreme virtue. Christianity is a religion of martyrs and confessors, of men and women who believe that their faith in God is worth living and dying for.

Thank you, Jesus, for loving me with such passion! Thank you for calling me into existence and for choosing me to be your disciple, granting me the priceless gift of faith in you! Who am I, after all, that you should love me so much? Who am I that you should pursue me with such ardor? Who am I that you should die for me on the cross? Yet you do and you have! The only way I can repay you is to love you and love souls in the same way.

**Sacred Heart of Jesus, consumed with passionate love,
make my heart more like yours!**

Tuesday—Week Two

If anyone wishes to be first, he shall be the
last of all and the servant of all.

—*Mark 9:35*, NAB

. . .

In our modern world, education and sophistication are highly prized commodities. We assume that the more degrees and titles someone has, the greater that person is and the better he or she grasps the true meaning of human life. But how impressed was Jesus with the "wisdom of the world"?

Not much, it would seem. In fact, his idea of greatness took an altogether different tack. When an argument over which of them was the most important broke out among the disciples, Jesus told them that whoever wanted to be first must be last—and the servant of all. Interestingly, Jesus doesn't seem to mind that the apostles were ambitious. He doesn't reproach them for desiring greatness or for wanting to be all they could be. Instead, he invites them to set their sights higher still, to where true greatness lies.

But the paradox is that, in order to go higher, they need to go lower. Jesus' model for greatness is a small child, with no rank and no accomplishments to his name (cf. Mark 9:37). Jesus tells us that if we really wish to be something, we need to choose the last place and become servants of our brothers and sisters.

Once again, Jesus doesn't just preach; he practices. He himself says that the Son of Man came into the world not to be served but to serve (cf. Matthew 20:28). This is what we see in his day-to-day life. There's nothing wrong with fame or human accomplishments. Like the apostles, however, we need to learn that there is a higher form of greatness to esteem and aspire to. On Judgment Day, we won't be asked about our degrees or our human achievements. We will be examined about love.

Thank you, Jesus, for your moving example of servanthood. Help me to acquire a servant's heart like yours. I want to focus less on worldly opinion and more on what is important in your eyes, on what you consider to be great. I know there is a lot of this greatness around me—simple people who live beautiful lives, hidden in their daily fidelity and salt-of-the-earth goodness. Give me a servant's heart too, like theirs and like yours!

**Sacred Heart of Jesus, servant of all,
make my heart more like yours!**

WEDNESDAY—WEEK TWO

For you know the grace of our Lord Jesus Christ, that
though he was rich, yet for your sake he became poor,
so that by his poverty you might become rich.

—*2 Corinthians 8:9*

. . .

By all accounts, Jesus was poor. He was born in a borrowed stable, lived in the Palestinian boondocks, often slept on the ground, ate what was set before him, and was buried in somebody else's tomb. Yet Jesus didn't choose material poverty for its own sake or because he wanted to belong to the proletariat. He did so because his heart was poor. It was detached from all the "things" we humans so readily crave and cling to. Because his heart was poor, Jesus was truly free.

The funny thing is, we think that the more we have the freer we will be, but usually the opposite is true. We so easily become possessed by what we possess. We serve things instead of letting them serve us. Jesus never fell into that trap.

At the same time, Jesus never despised material things. He used what he had without ever setting his heart on it. He taught that there are many forms of poverty. The truly poor person is the one who is far from God. The truly rich man is the one with God in his heart. Jesus gave us God. He revealed to us the Father's love, and in this way he offered us all "a share in his riches."[1]

Jesus, thank you for your example of poverty. The absence of many things in your life didn't make you glum, it just made you peaceful. You didn't spend your time running around chasing after possessions. You used your time and attention for greater things. Because you weren't attached to material things, you had more time for prayer and service. In my own life, keep me poor in the midst of the world, so that I use things but love only you!

**Sacred Heart of Jesus, familiar with poverty,
make my heart more like yours!**

1. From the preface for the Eucharistic Prayer, Weekdays I.

THURSDAY—WEEK TWO

Foxes have holes, and birds of the air have nests; but
the Son of Man has nowhere to lay his head.
—*Luke 9:58*

. . .

Jesus invites his followers to opt for a detached, uncluttered life as he
did. When a scribe approached him and said, "Teacher, I will follow
you wherever you go," Jesus didn't answer, "Great! Glad to have you on
board!" He first wanted to make sure that the man knew what he was in
for, and so Jesus tells him that, though foxes have holes and birds have
nests, he himself has nowhere to lay his head.

In following Jesus, we also must accept his conditions, and one of
these is detachment. He reminds us that we are pilgrims passing through,
with no lasting city in this world. He invites us to the simplicity of an
uncluttered life and, even more important, an uncluttered heart! He
wants us free of attachments to things that will only distract us or take
God's place in our lives. He doesn't want our hearts to be complicated
with cobwebs, hidden cupboards, dark corners, or cubbyholes. Sweep it.
Clean it. Let the light of Christ illuminate everything.

We worry about many, many things, yet Jesus assures us that only one
is truly necessary. Peace is found not in an abundance of goods but in an
uncluttered heart devoted to the Lord.

My heart isn't as free as yours, Lord Jesus. If I am honest, I see that I am attached to many things, material and immaterial. I care too much about having nice things, what people think of me, and where I will go on vacation. These "harmless" little attachments clutter my heart and disturb my peace of mind. Help me to deal with the physical realities of life responsibly but without ever setting my heart on them.

**Sacred Heart of Jesus, free of clutter,
make my heart more like yours!**

Friday—Week Two

Abba, Father.

—*Mark 14:36*

. . .

• •

You might think that, being God, Jesus would have been pretty self-sufficient. There wasn't much he *couldn't* do, after all. He walked on water, cured lepers, calmed storms, and even raised the dead. So why pray? What need could Jesus possibly have had to talk to God?

Jesus revealed a God who was a trinity of persons, a community rather than an isolated individual. As a man, Jesus lived this communion with his Father especially through prayer. When he went off to the mountain or the desert, he wasn't "lost in his own thoughts" but immersed in conversation with his Father. He loved his Father, and he loved to spend time with him. For Jesus, prayer wasn't a chore he had to get out of the way but a delight, an activity he looked forward to. He made time for prayer because for him it was a priority.

In short, Jesus didn't pray just because he "had" to. He didn't turn to God just as a problem-solver or a bodyguard. He turned to him as a *Father*. It would be a shame if the only time we dealt with our father was when we needed to borrow the car keys or take out a short-term loan! This wasn't Jesus' attitude. He bounced ideas off God, shared his innermost thoughts and aspirations with him, and sometimes just enjoyed his company without saying anything at all. The heart of Jesus was indeed a prayerful heart.

Lord, help me to appreciate prayer. Help me to be more grateful for the honor of being able to speak with you every day, knowing that you hear me, that you love me, that you enjoy our time together. Everything looks different from the perspective of prayer, because it is your perspective on things from heaven. Teach me to pray as you prayed!

***Sacred Heart of Jesus, ever prayerful,
make my heart more like yours!***

SATURDAY—WEEK TWO

Get behind me, Satan! You are an obstacle to me; for you
are thinking not as God does, but as human beings do.
—*Mark 16:36,* NAB

. . .

When Jesus began talking about his Passion and explaining that he
would have to go to Jerusalem to suffer and be put to death, Peter was
aghast. He tried to convince Jesus that this was an awful plan. Jesus'
response came in those terrible words, "Get behind me, Satan!" Jesus
loved Peter, but he didn't let his affection for him hinder the fulfillment
of God's plan. What Peter was proposing might seem very attractive, but
Jesus saw it as a temptation, and he reacted fiercely. Peter was suggesting
that Jesus not accept the cross, that he find an easier way. But that was
not the Father's will.

Jesus was incredibly radical when it came to God's will. He didn't
allow negotiations with other possibilities. God's will was not one possible option among many but the only road. Jesus recommends the same
radicalness to his disciples. "If your right eye causes you to sin, pluck
it out and throw it away" (Matthew 5:29). This wasn't the common-
ground, have-your-cake-and-eat-it-too approach. It was the yes-or-no,
with-me-or-against-me approach.

We are used to compromise in our lives. In a democratic society, there
is a necessary give-and-take. This works well in most areas of our life,
but Jesus shows us that there is one area where no compromise should
be accepted: God's will. No matter what the cost, no matter what we
may have to lose or give up, nothing should stand in the way of what the
Father asks of us. This is the road to holiness.

Lord, thank you for your example of radicalness. You show me that some things are worth fighting for, even dying for. Let me love God's will above all other things. He wants only good things for me, and even when I don't see clearly, help me trust in his wisdom. Let me call temptation by its name and unmask the enemy of my soul, no matter what guise he puts on.

Sacred Heart of Jesus, radically committed to God's will, make my heart more like yours!

Week Three

During the third week of Lent, we will contemplate the purity, simplicity, wisdom, and joy of the Heart of Jesus. We realize more and more how well-rounded Jesus' personality was. He truly exemplified every virtue, including those that you and I most need to work on, and so he is a model—the best model—for each of us. We get to know him best by spending time with him, listening to him, and allowing him to mold us into true Christians.

Lord Jesus, thank you for these fruitful first weeks of Lent and for the many graces you have been giving me—those I can see and those I cannot. Make me, in turn, an instrument of your grace and of your mercy for others. The more I am like you, and the more I allow you to work in and through me, the more others will discover the love you have for them as well. This is my prayer! Amen.

SUNDAY—WEEK THREE

As you, Father, are in me and I in you,
that they also may be in us.
—*John 17:21,* NAB

. . .

· ·

At the Last Supper, Jesus asked the Father that we, his followers, might enjoy with him the same type of intimacy that he shared with the Father. Jesus assures us that he wills this level of communion with us. He doesn't want anything to separate us or stand in the way of our total union with him. He invites us into communion with the Blessed Trinity, into the deep intimacy that he lives with the Father and the Holy Spirit. This is undoubtedly a lot for us to even begin to understand, but we should try. It tells us a lot about who we are and who we were meant to be.

Prayer can be hard work. It requires perseverance and effort. But it is an exercise that can change our lives. God doesn't intend to settle for a mere platonic relationship with us, or a passing acquaintance. He wants our close friendship. He wants our intimacy. He wants our trust. He wants our company. Prayer can be a foretaste of heaven, an experience of union with God. Like Jesus, we need to make time to devote to God. Prayer doesn't just happen; we need to make it happen. There is no better use of our time.

Lord, I understand the value of prayer in theory, but in practice I often find it difficult. Sometimes I don't see that it changes very much. Thank you for your example, Lord! In the midst of your countless activities, you found an extraordinary amount of time to spend with your Father. You liked to be with him and made him your active confidant. You spoke with him of your most personal thoughts, frustrations, doubts, and ideals. Help me to enjoy the same intimate communion with the Father and with you!

*Sacred Heart of Jesus, intimately one with the Father,
make my heart more like yours!*

MONDAY—WEEK THREE

Blessed are the pure in heart.
—*Matthew 5:8*

. . .

In emphasizing purity of heart, Jesus isn't taking away from the importance of being pure in mind and body as well, but he underscores the heart once again as the center of our being. It is above all our *love* that must be pure, untainted by anything unworthy.

What is purity? It is the absence of foreign elements that would corrupt or diminish the authenticity of something. Pure, twenty-four-carat gold contains no such foreign elements. It is unmingled, unalloyed, and unadulterated. What you see is what you get. The same can be said for pure single-malt Scotch whiskey, pure maple syrup, or pure cashmere. They are all 100 percent what they claim to be. Nothing added.

Purity means authenticity. It has nothing to do with prudery or Puritanism or hatred of the human body. This authenticity is what we see throughout Jesus' life. He was pure in heart not just because he was celibate. His heart was pure because he loved truly, without self-interest or second intentions. He looked at others not as objects from whom he could derive some gain but as persons to be loved. He didn't love people to please himself but loved them for their own sake. And that's why Jesus' gaze didn't bring shame or embarrassment but instead a sense of security and peace.

This purity of heart is the sort of purity to which we are called. It isn't easy, because self-interest always seems to worm its way into our relationships, despite our best efforts to keep it out. Even when our primary motive is good, we often discover secondary motives that are not so noble. The human heart requires constant purification. Examining

43

our conscience helps us to unearth the impurities that can stain our love. But we also need the purifying power of God's grace, the fire of his love.

Lord, I so admire the purity of your Sacred Heart. You were able to love so intensely, so passionately, and yet so purely. I want a clean heart like yours, a heart cleansed of pettiness, lusts, clinginess, greed, envy, grudges, complexes, and bitterness. Let me love purely, which is to love truly and authentically.

Sacred Heart of Jesus, pure and clean of heart,
make my heart more like yours!

TUESDAY—WEEK THREE

For the foolishness of God is wiser than men, and
the weakness of God is stronger than men.
—*1 Corinthians 1:25*

. . .

•••

St. Paul incisively distinguished between the wisdom of the world and
true Christian wisdom. The Christian understanding of wisdom goes
beyond mere cleverness, sophistication, education, or data accumula-
tion. Indeed, this worldly, two-dimensional sort of wisdom merely "puffs
up" without building anything lasting (cf. 1 Corinthians 8:1). Christian
wisdom goes beyond mere facts and information. It deals with *meaning*
and *value*. This is the wisdom Jesus possessed in abundance.

Wisdom, according to Pope Benedict, seeks to understand what matters. Whereas knowing many things may be useful, it is nothing without
wisdom. Wisdom, says Benedict, "is knowledge of the essential, knowledge of the aim of our life and of how we should live."[1] Unlike mere
cleverness, wisdom sees clearly the difference between what is important
and what is not.

Jesus' heart was wise, not just because he possessed a bounty of knowledge but because he understood the worth of things. He immediately
saw what mattered and distinguished it from what was unimportant
or useless. Once again, one of the most compelling aspects of Jesus'
teaching is how it is reflected in his own life. Jesus' own scale of values
mirrored the lessons he offered to the crowds. He told us to pay little
attention to things like food and clothing and to focus instead on justice, mercy, and his kingdom.

1. Benedict XVI, homily, August 30, 2009.

Christ's teaching and witness of wisdom proves particularly consoling to those whose lives are filled with thousands of daily chores and little opportunity for ongoing education and academic pursuits. Christian wisdom is accessible to everyone, from taxi drivers to homemakers to CEOs. Paying attention to what matters and disregarding what doesn't fills the heart with a wisdom that doesn't require a PhD.

Lord, you never went to college and yet you are the teacher of humanity. At the age of twelve, you were already seated among the learned. You are wise because you possess the only knowledge that matters in the end: knowledge of God and the meaning of human existence. Help me to adjust my way of thinking to yours; teach me to be wise like you.

Sacred Heart of Jesus, full of wisdom,
make my heart more like yours!

WEDNESDAY—WEEK THREE

These things I have spoken to you, that my joy
may be in you, and that your joy may be full.
—*John 15:11*

. . .

• •

Jesus came to offer us the fullness of life. He saw us enslaved and came as our liberator. He saw us lost and came to show us the way home. He saw us confused and brought us the truth. He saw us lonely and forsaken and came to show us the Father's love. But he also came to bring us joy. He saw us sad, frustrated, anxious, and fearful and came to share his own happiness with us.

It's true that the Gospels don't offer instances of Jesus breaking into fits of laughter, playing pranks on the apostles, or telling jokes around the campfire. At the same time, the portrait we get from the Gospels tells of a joyful heart, drawing those around him to discover what he had inside. People were happy to be with Jesus because his own interior joy was contagious. In the midst of so many travails, with the weight of the world's salvation on his shoulders, he found the greatest joy in the realization that, no matter what, nothing could ever separate him from the Father's love.

If our hearts are to be like Christ's, they must be filled with this same joy. Sulkiness and Christianity have never gone well together, borne out by St. Teresa's saying that "a sad saint is a sorry saint." Our deep joy reveals the authenticity of our encounter with the risen Lord and becomes an invitation to others to discover what we have found.

Lord Jesus, how I would have loved to meet you here on earth! Your personality was so attractive, your character so magnetizing, that everyone wanted to be with you. Above all, I would have liked to experience the deep joy that filled you. I would have liked to see your smile. Teach me to smile like that, to offer your smile to the world. Make me an apostle of joy, Lord. In a world filled with anguish and vanity, people hunger and thirst for the joy that only you can give. Let joy be the gift I offer to others and to you as well, since you love a cheerful giver!

**Sacred Heart of Jesus, truly joyful,
make my heart more like yours!**

THURSDAY—WEEK THREE

I thank you, Father.

—*Matthew 11:25*

. . .

As children, we learn that courtesy and politeness are important, and they characterize us as well mannered. As life goes on, however, we realize that true gratitude goes much deeper than mere courtesy. It is a virtue of the heart and a very rare one at that.

In Jesus' dealings, especially with God, he exhibits the virtue of gratitude over and over. Before he heals Lazarus, he thanks God for hearing him. He gives thanks before every meal, and he thanks God for revealing to little ones what is hidden from the learned and the clever (cf. Luke 10:21). We sometimes think that God's blessings are to be expected, but Jesus never took them for granted. He took the time to thank God because he had a grateful heart.

In his dealings with us too, Jesus is just as grateful. During his earthly life as well as now, he is deeply grateful for every gesture of love and every act of kindness. Nothing is lost on him. Knowing how much our gratitude pleases the heart of Christ, there are many ways we can grow in this virtue daily. The little kindnesses all around us, which we so easily take for granted, furnish us with constant opportunities to thank. The humbler we are and the more aware that we are unworthy of the many gifts we daily receive, the easier we will find it to practice this beautiful quality of Jesus' heart.

Lord, I am often more aware of the good things I do for others than of the good things they do for me. I tend to expect people to treat me well. I also take God's many gifts to me for granted. Let me start right now to thank you as you deserve. Thank you for being with me now, for listening to me, for being my Savior and best friend!

**Sacred Heart of Jesus, sincerely grateful,
make my heart more like yours!**

FRIDAY—WEEK THREE

I live by faith in the Son of God, who
loved me and gave himself for me.

—*Galatians 2:20*

. . .

• •

If the human heart symbolizes anything, it symbolizes love. Jesus' heart too, despite its many other qualities and virtues, stands above all for his love. The qualities and virtues we have been considering in the pages of this book are really all facets of Christ's love. Christ's love is personal, passionate, enduring, heroic, and eternal. Lent is an ideal time to contemplate that love, experience that love, and respond to that love.

When we read God's Word, we should form the habit of looking not just at Jesus' words and actions—the story of his life. On every page, we should stop and ask ourselves *why*. Why the Incarnation? Why the birth in a poor stable in Bethlehem? Why the Last Supper? Why the agony in the garden? Why the Passion? Why the cross? Why the resurrection? The answer to all these and all the other whys of Christ's life is always the same: because he loved me. He *loves* me. Every page of the Gospels is a testament to Jesus' love for me.

To contemplate the heart of Jesus is to contemplate his love. When Jesus revealed his Sacred Heart to St. Margaret Mary, the first thing he said was, "*Behold this heart.*" Look at him. Contemplate him. What a difference it would make in our lives if we simply lived with an ongoing awareness of Christ's love for us!

Dearest Jesus, thank you for your love for me! Thank you for becoming man and for living and dying for me. Let me never forget this! Let me never become hardened to this central truth of my entire existence. You love me!

No matter what befalls me, no matter what direction my life takes, you will always be there with your love for me. You are my strength, my consolation, my all!

**Sacred Heart of Jesus, bursting with love,
make my heart more like yours!**

SATURDAY—WEEK THREE

Let the children come to me.

—*Matthew 19:14*

. . .

Jesus is rightly considered the greatest teacher who ever lived. His wisdom went beyond that of Socrates or Plato, Confucius or Einstein. Yet, despite the undeniable depth of his message, he taught with astonishing simplicity. Most of his teaching took the form of parables—simple stories that even the uneducated could understand. He made the message of salvation accessible to everyone, the learned and unlearned alike.

Jesus himself is as simple as simple can be—no special titles, no degrees, no dignities, no rank. He's just a teacher from a small town, busy saving the world. He is comfortable with rich and poor, men and women, adults and children, politicians and fishermen. He doesn't require an appointment to speak with him. He inspires confidence and closeness because his heart is simple.

People don't wait on Jesus hand and foot. No royal court surrounds him, and no secret-service men keep people away from him. He doesn't set up shop on the upper floor of a Jerusalem office suite to await elite visitors. Instead, he goes out to meet people, to listen, to heal, to serve. This is the simplicity that marks his heart and his life.

Alas, we often aren't like this. We still associate greatness with worldly renown, celebrity status, athletic prowess, or impressive achievements. Rarely would we look at a little child and spontaneously think, "Ah! I am in the presence of true greatness!" We could use a good dose of Christlike simplicity to balance the importance we put on earthly opinions and standards.

Lord, I live in a world that has a strange set of values. Things that are worthless in your sight are prized highly, and things that you admire are scoffed at or ignored. I sometimes get caught up between these two worlds, although I want to be fully "Christian" in my outlook. You call me to live in this world but without being caught up in it. Thank you for your example of simplicity. Help me to develop a simple heart!

Sacred Heart of Jesus, simple and childlike, make my heart more like yours!

Week Four

Jesus spent forty days in the desert before beginning his public mission, during which time—the Gospels tell us—he fasted and underwent temptation. A prayer marathon, like any marathon, gets progressively harder as one nears the end, and a person's energy and resolve can begin to flag. Yet Jesus admirably saw it through. We too in our lenten marathon need to keep up our enthusiasm for prayer and spiritual exercise as we draw closer to Holy Week. The rewards are a closer friendship with our Lord and a deeper sharing in his work of salvation.

Dearest Jesus, you once said that when a person lays his hand to the plow, he should never look back (cf. Luke 9:62). You gave me a perfect example of this. You persevered in your mission till the end, even through terrible suffering, out of love for me. Help me to persevere in my good intentions and resolutions so that they bear all the fruit that you intend for me. Let every day of Lent bring me closer and closer to you, my treasure and my dearest Friend. Amen.

SUNDAY—WEEK FOUR

As long as the day lasts I must carry out the work of the one
who sent me; the night will soon be here when no one can
work. As long as I am in the world I am the light of the world.
—*John 9:4–5*, JB

. . .

As Jesus approaches his Passion, he demonstrates his power even more
brilliantly, both by his words and by his actions. He performs amazing
miracles, like healing a man who was born blind. He boldly calls himself
"the light of the world." His miracles reveal God's power at work within
him, and the Gospels tell us again and again that Jesus is truly the fullness of God, bringing light to our dark world.

Just as he did with this blind man, Jesus wants to touch our lives—not
only our bodies but our spirits too. He manifests God's grace to us in
human, everyday ways, and he wants us to have confidence and hope.
Jesus' healing acts aren't meant merely to impress or amaze; what he is
really after is a personal encounter, one that includes all facets of our
humanity: body, mind, and spirit. In everything he did, he used all the
means at his disposal to bring our humanity to its fullness.

The light of Christ continues to be revealed today through his sacraments: the waters of baptism, the priest's healing words during confes-
sion, the bread and wine of Holy Communion are all ways that Christ's
light touches us. The closer we are to Jesus, the more clearly we see.
When we draw close to the light, everything becomes brighter and
clearer.

This is how we can embrace our earthly existence. We are physical
beings, not angels. The physical realities around us can be important
signposts to direct our hearts toward the spiritual realities that fill us
with light and gladness.

Jesus, you are the light of my life. In the midst of the dark days you faced on earth, you shone brightly, and you illuminate the dark places in my own life. You are the light of the world, and you are stronger than any darkness I might face. This Lent, let me be even more conscious of this, especially through the sacraments of penance and the Eucharist.

**Sacred Heart of Jesus, light of the world,
make my heart more like yours!**

MONDAY—WEEK FOUR

Ask and you will receive.

—*Luke 11:9*, NAB

. . .

We sometimes resist asking God for favors because we unconsciously think we need to "save up" our requests for something more important, as if God were a genie who grants only three wishes. So, instead of bothering God with our little needs and aspirations, we often wait until some really important crisis occurs before we "use up" our petitions. Somehow we think this improves our chances of receiving an answer.

What was Jesus' attitude toward divine requests? He encouraged his followers to ask for things from God. He tells us to ask, to seek, and to knock, and he promises that we will be heard and answered. He spurs us to boldness of faith, to believe that we have already received what we are asking for (cf. Mark 11:24). And if God should seem to tarry, Jesus recommends that we "wear him out" by asking over and over until we get satisfaction (cf. Luke 18:1–8).

At the same time, Jesus also reminds us that God "knows what you need before you ask him" (Matthew 6:8), so in our requests we don't have to be exhaustive for fear of forgetting something. We're not "informing" God about our needs and desires; we are expressing them and asking for his intervention.

Jesus prayed all the time. He prayed in public and in private, aloud and silently. We find him praising God and thanking him, but we also see him asking God for what he needs, most poignantly in the Garden of Gethsemane, where he begs his Father to let this cup pass (cf. Luke 22:42). He reveals to us a God who *wants* to be asked, a Father who *delights* in us approaching him with our requests. He already knows what we need—he just likes to hear it coming from us.

It helps me, Lord, to remember that God wants me to ask him for things. He delights in my requests and in being able to come to my assistance when I call on him. I'm not a burden to him but a joy. Let me always praise and thank you, Lord—but let me also make many requests, even for simple things. Let me place all my cares in God's hands.

**Sacred Heart of Jesus, bold in prayer,
make my heart more like yours!**

Tuesday—Week Four

I have compassion on the crowd.

—*Mark 8:2*

. . .

All of us have moments when we've had enough. When the in-laws have overstayed their welcome, or the kids have gone beyond the limit and are misbehaving, or the job has become so stressful that we can't wait for the clock to strike five, we need some downtime. We just want to be left alone to recharge our batteries. We love our fellow man, of course, but enough is enough! At the end of the day, when we are tired of taking care of everyone else's needs, we would like everyone to just go home.

Being human like us, Jesus must have experienced the same thing. From time to time he must have reached the end of his rope. Yet, even though he must have felt the same frustration, fatigue, and exhaustion that we do, he didn't seem to put any limits on his generosity. And the reason? He had a truly *compassionate* heart. He cared deeply about people and did everything in his power to assist them, despite the sacrifice that required.

Jesus truly felt other people's pain. Their sorrows were his sorrows. This is what *com-passion* means—the ability to share another's suffering. But Jesus' compassion was also "active." He felt pity for others, but he also worked to alleviate it, as when he provided food for the large crowd who had been following him for three days.

How do we react to others' pain? Are we so wrapped up in our own concerns that we are practically oblivious to the needs of others? If we allow Christ to teach us, we may be surprised at what he tells us. An open heart is the beginning of a compassionate, Christlike heart.

Thank you, Lord, for your example of compassion. My own heart so easily gravitates to myself and my own interests. So many times I don't really want to be bothered with others' concerns. That needs to change. If I am truly to have a heart like yours, it must become more selfless and compassionate.

**Sacred Heart of Jesus, full of compassion,
make my heart more like yours!**

WEDNESDAY—WEEK FOUR

I know mine and mine know me.

—John 10:14, NAB

. . .

The Peanuts character Linus once quipped, "I love mankind; it's *people* I can't stand."[1] This sentiment could be applied to many of us. It's much easier to love *humanity* than it is to love the greasy guy coughing next to you on the bus, or the driver who cuts you off on the road. Mankind as a group is one thing, but when we get down to the nuts and bolts of real human beings with all their quirks and foibles, love becomes far more demanding.

What about God? We know that he loves "mankind." We know that he so loved "the world" that he sent his only Son to be its savior. But do we really believe that he loves our grumpy neighbor or a smelly street person?

When we take a look at Jesus, we discover a good shepherd who knows each of his sheep by name. We find a shepherd for whom every individual sheep is so important that he would leave ninety-nine in the wilderness to seek out one that strayed. For Jesus, human beings were never numbers; they were always persons. Every person was irreplaceable; all were of infinite worth to him.

To have a heart like Christ's means to have a heart that sees every human being as precious. It means a personal touch in our dealings with others, even if they are "only" the checkout clerk at the grocery store or the shampoo girl at the hair salon. Loving all humanity must translate into loving the person next to me right now.

Jesus, thank you for the way you love each of us personally. Teach me to see each person I encounter through your eyes and with your heart. Let me love people one by one, without excluding anyone. Help me to look beyond their defects and see the beauty of your image in all of them.

Sacred Heart of Jesus, imbued with personal love, make my heart more like yours!

1. Robert L. Short, *The Gospel According to Peanuts* (Louisville: Wesminster John Knox Press, 2000).

THURSDAY—WEEK FOUR

For this I was born and for this I came into the
world, to testify to the truth. Everyone who
belongs to the truth listens to my voice.

—*John 18:37,* NAB

. . .

No one likes to get "played." We like people to be straight with us, to tell us the truth, and to call a spade a spade. Jesus felt the same abhorrence for dishonesty, hypocrisy, and duplicity. He himself was always truthful. More than that, he was "the truth" (John 14:6).

Jesus didn't invent fables to get us to behave. He tells only the truth about God, about judgment, about human nature, about heaven and hell, about the meaning of life. We can trust him because, no matter what the consequences, he never lied. There is something deeply comforting about a person who will always tell you the truth. Jesus is like that. We can count on him always to tell us the truth, whether it be tough or easy for us to hear. And yet he also does so with love: *caritas in veritate*.

Jesus assures us that the truth "will set us free" (John 8:32). It sets us free in the first place because it liberates us from error and false notions about God and ourselves. Ignorance is always a sort of slavery, especially when we're illiterate about the things that matter most—the meaning of life, where we come from, and where we are going. But the truth sets us free also because the person who lives in the truth lives in light, both inside and outside. This person is transparent and authentic. Duplicity slowly corrodes and darkens the soul, whereas integrity—living according to the truth—makes one freer and freer.

Jesus lived the deepest integrity known to humanity. There were no divisions in his personality. He didn't have a professional side and a personal side—he simply was who he was. We are called to live the same sort of integrity, ordering all our words and actions according to our deepest beliefs. We are called to be a light for others, shining truth where there is only darkness, ignorance, and sin.

Jesus, thank you for always telling me the truth. Thank you for your witness of honesty and integrity. Not many in this world of ours truly practice what they preach. I have been let down so many times by people I've counted on, but never by you. I too have been called to bear witness to the truth both through my words and through my actions. May the same integrity that filled your heart fill mine as well.

**Sacred Heart of Jesus, honest and truthful,
make my heart more like yours!**

FRIDAY—WEEK FOUR

When the days drew near for him to be received
up, he set his face to go to Jerusalem.

—*Luke 9:51*

· · ·

We sometimes think of Jesus as being inexorably drawn by fate toward his Passion and death. He seems almost like a victim—albeit a willing one—of destiny, without much say in the matter. It is easy to undervalue the courage it took for him to be faithful. Yet Jesus assures us that no one took his life from him—he gave it up of his own accord (see John 10:18). He met death head-on, for love of us.

His Passion and death provide the best example of this courageous heart, but we see it all through his life. He was courageous when he had to leave his childhood home and beloved mother to begin his public mission. He was courageous when he had to face hostile crowds, who on one occasion even sought to throw him off a cliff. He was courageous when he taught the undiluted truth despite the negative consequences. He was courageous when arguing with the scribes and Pharisees, knowing they were plotting his death. And yes, he was courageous before the Sanhedrin, before Herod, before Pontius Pilate, and before his executioners. He never fled from hardship or persecution or sacrifice. Because he had such remarkable courage, nothing and no one would change his course.

Courage is often undervalued in the Christian life. Yet when we fail to accomplish the good we set out to do, isn't it often not because we don't want to but because we lack courage when obstacles appear? Often it is fear that paralyzes our good intentions and makes them sterile and fruitless. We don't pray because it's hard and we see no results. We don't ask pardon for our sins because we lack the courage to face up to them. We don't persevere in our good resolutions because to do so requires sacrifice. And we don't follow Jesus too closely because it means embracing the cross. If only we had more courage!

Jesus, the courage you manifested goes beyond what I feel capable of. The ideal is so high I fear I can't reach it. It almost seems that I need courage just to want to be courageous! I have so many fears, so many doubts, so much timidity where I should have strength. I know the key is a deeper union with you so that I don't think of myself apart from you, as if I were just imitating you and your example. You really want to live in me—I want that too. I need your grace; I need your courage!

Sacred Heart of Jesus, resolutely courageous,
make my heart more like yours!

SATURDAY—WEEK FOUR

I lay down my life, that I may take it again. No one
takes it from me, but I lay it down of my own accord.
I have power to lay it down, and I have power to take
it again; this charge I have received from my Father.

—*John 10:17–18*

. . .

Jesus was faithful not because he had no choice but because he chose to
be faithful. In his perfect obedience to the Father's will, he never felt as
if he were just going through the motions. Whereas some Christians can
feel shackled by their faith and burdened by the moral standards they
are asked to meet, Jesus never seemed to experience this. For Jesus, the
Father's will was liberating, not enslaving.

Jesus wanted us to understand that his sacrifice was free. He seemed
to revel in his freedom. He chose to give his life for us, out of love for
us and for the Father. That's why, in the Garden of Gethsemane, when
Peter steps forward to defend Jesus from the guards who have come to
take him into custody, Jesus tells him to put away his sword. He asks
Peter, "Do you think that I cannot appeal to my Father, and he will at
once send me more than twelve legions of angels?" (Matthew 26:53).
In other words, if he was captured, it's because he allowed himself to be
captured. At any moment he could have called it off. At any moment he
could have said no.

Jesus' absolute freedom underscores his personal power. He could
have walked away, but he didn't. We too are free. We too can say yes or
no to God. We too can escape many difficulties and inconveniences if
we choose to. But with God's grace, we can also be faithful regardless
of the cost.

Lord, the more I study your life, the more impressed I am by the completeness of your character. The better I get to know you, the more I appreciate the beauty of virtue as you revealed and lived it. You make me love you more, and you make me want to be like you. You showed that true freedom and power of choice are the result of being one with the Father, doing his will no matter what. Love makes us supremely free.

Sacred Heart of Jesus, truly free,
make my heart more like yours!

Week Five

In this final week before Holy Week, we contemplate Jesus as a man of prayer, of self-discipline, of mercy, and of loving obedience. We continue to discover new facets and nuances to the Heart of Christ, our model for being truly human, as God created us to be. As we open our own hearts to him, we reveal our wounds and imperfections, and we allow the divine physician to heal us and remold our hearts in his image and likeness. Let us offer him this next week with generosity and love.

Lord Jesus, here I am, still by your side, where I wish to be always. No matter where you are—on the mountains, by the sea, on the road, or on the cross—I want to be there with you. Let my contemplation of the virtues of your heart increase my love for you and inspire me to want to be more and more like you. Purify me from my many imperfections. Heart of Jesus, in you I trust! Amen.

SUNDAY—WEEK FIVE

Now is my soul troubled. And what shall I say? "Father,
save me from this hour"? No, for this purpose I have
come to this hour. Father, glorify your name.

—John 12:27–28

. . .

• •

As Jesus' Passion draws closer, he knows exactly what awaits him. "His
hour" has arrived. He will suffer betrayal by one of his closest friends,
denial from his most trusted disciple, abandonment by his dearest com-
panions, rejection by those he has come to redeem, and public humilia-
tion. He will endure the most horrific physical torture, and he will also
experience a kind of separation from his Father. And then he will die a
painful and lonely death.

But knowing all this, he tells his disciples that he is going to suffer it
all willingly for God's glory and the salvation of souls. He is motivated
by the strongest love imaginable, a love that enables him to obey God
under the most troubling circumstances. He has always told his listeners
that if they wanted to truly follow him, they would have to take up their
cross daily (cf. Luke 9:23). Now, as the events of the Passion are about
to unfold, Jesus says, "Unless a grain of wheat falls into the earth and
dies, it remains alone; but if it dies, it bears much fruit" (John 12:24).

Christ continues to pour out his life for others on the cross, giving
himself unselfishly for the salvation of souls and for their good. Our
lives too must bear the same sign of the cross—we too are called to be
self-giving and self-sacrificing for the good of others. If we really want
to "see" Christ, we only have to look at him dying on the cross and he
will give us true life. This Lent, may our reflecting on the crucifix reveal

an even deeper understanding of all that Christ's sacrifice accomplished, and at what price!

Jesus, you suffered so much on my behalf! You carried your cross willingly out of pure love, while I so often resist mine. I carry my little crosses so reluctantly, so halfheartedly. If it were up to me, I would choose a path without any suffering at all. But you chose to suffer willingly. Help me, Lord, to be rid of the selfishness that clings so tightly to me. Help me to embrace out of love for you whatever crosses I face. Let my "death to self" bear much fruit for your kingdom!

**Sacred Heart of Jesus, suffering for me,
make my heart more like yours!**

MONDAY—WEEK FIVE

I came not to call the righteous, but sinners.
—*Matthew 9:13*

. . .

In the Gospels, Jesus talks about both judgment and mercy. He assures us that there will be a final reckoning and that we will have to give an accounting for our actions. On the other hand, he also assures us that mercy is available for even the worst sinners and that he came to take away our sins rather than condemn us for them. In the cross, justice and mercy kiss because Jesus takes justice upon himself, receiving what we deserve and giving us what we do not deserve. And so the prophet Isaiah's words are fulfilled: "With his stripes we are healed" (Isaiah 53:5). In the end, love triumphs, and it does so under the form of mercy.

Perhaps the most touching example of this came at the end of Jesus' life, as he hung on the cross, between heaven and earth, his blood and breath slowly escaping his body. While one of the two thieves who are crucified with Jesus complains bitterly and taunts Jesus, the other turns to him to rebuke him. He recognizes that both are getting their just deserts, whereas Jesus has done nothing wrong. The good thief then turns to Jesus and utters the most important words of his entire life: "Jesus, remember me when you come into your kingdom" (Luke 23:42, *NAB*). Who knows what he expected to hear in reply, but it couldn't have been more marvelous than the response he received. Without hesitating, Jesus simply said, "Truly, I say to you, today you will be with me in Paradise" (Luke 23:43).

When, perhaps rightly, we feel indignation and even anger toward sinners who hurt others and disturb the social order, before we consign them to hell we should ask ourselves, "Would I be willing to die for him?

Do I, like Christ, find no pleasure in his punishment but desire above all else his conversion?" Where would we be without that mercy? Would you really like to be judged simply on your own merits? I wouldn't. All of us have desperate need of God's mercy, whether we realize it or not.

Jesus, when I look at your life, I am moved by your great mercy. You felt the effects of sin in your own flesh, and yet you are the first to excuse, to pardon, to welcome back into your friendship. Praised be your gentle, merciful heart!

> **Sacred Heart of Jesus, rich in mercy,**
> **make my heart more like yours!**

TUESDAY—WEEK FIVE

Rising very early before dawn, he left and went
off to a deserted place, where he prayed.

—*Mark 1:35,* NAB

. . .

Since Jesus was not just a man but also God, we readily assume that
things had to be easier for him than they are for us. After all, we think,
how tough could it have been if he was really God? In these lenten
meditations on the Sacred Heart of Christ, we should remember that
his humanity was not an act. He didn't just "go through the motions"
of being human like us. He really was. All the aches and pains, all the
trials and tribulations of weak humanity were Jesus' as well. That should
reassure us but also challenge us.

For example, Jesus got up long before dawn to pray by himself. For
those of us who sometimes have trouble getting up in the morning, this
should give us pause. It's not like Jesus just bounced out of bed, feeling
like a million bucks. Sometimes he woke up tired, sometimes he slept
badly on the uneven ground, sometimes he awoke with a headache or
a backache, and sometimes he surely felt like rolling over and sleeping
for a few more hours. This meditation isn't about Jesus' sleeping habits,
however; it's about his willpower. Jesus was disciplined in prayer, which
meant that often he did not what he felt like but what he knew he
should.

If it is to be fruitful, our prayer life demands more than good intentions. It requires discipline and selflessness; it requires constancy. And
most of all, it requires love. Love, and not some strange sense of "duty
for duty's sake," was the driving force behind Jesus' self-mastery. His
prayer life was urged on by love, driven by love. And he desires that our
times of prayer burn with the same holy love.

Jesus, fill my heart with a more profound love for you and for the many people I deal with each day. Give me a taste of your love, just a spark of the bonfire that is your Heart. Fill my heart with such a desire for prayer that no day will be complete without time spent alone with you!

**Sacred Heart of Jesus, constant in prayer,
make my heart more like yours!**

WEDNESDAY—WEEK FIVE

More tortuous than all else is the human heart,
beyond remedy; who can understand it?
—*Jeremiah 17:9*, NAB

. . .

The prophet Jeremiah, quoted above, expressed misgivings about undisciplined hearts. It's true that many people make bad decisions by "following their heart" rather than their head. Think, for example, of a young woman who, rather than listening to the warnings of good friends and even her own reason, marries an irresponsible playboy because she's "in love." Think of the poor guy who invests all his hard-earned savings in some fly-by-night venture, bedazzled by an unscrupulous con artist. By contrast, Jesus' heart was disciplined, so his decisions were not based on flights of fancy or the inclination of the moment but on deeper principles. His heart was well-ordered and governed by reason rather than at odds with it.

Jesus' grueling schedule and his ever present awareness that he was to suffer terribly and die for us on the cross demanded an incredible degree of self-discipline. Each day when he woke up, he knew he was one day closer to Calvary. Yet it wasn't stoicism that kept him on track; it was the deep love he bore for his Father and for each of us. His was a heart disciplined by love—and love, far from being at odds with discipline, requires it.

In today's society, discipline seems out of fashion, since people equate it with a lack of spontaneity and freedom. In Jesus' case, though, discipline made him not less flexible but more. Many of his most poignant encounters were "unplanned," and he always seemed to find time for everyone, despite his remarkably full schedule.

Our lives as well demand more than good intentions. Our prayer life, our family life, and our work life all require a disciplined heart. We need to stick with our resolutions and choose the best thing, not just what seems most fun or pleasing at the moment. How many times do we promise all sorts of things to God, only to see ourselves back in the same rut not long afterward? Don't we often suffer from a heart that lacks discipline? Jesus shows us that a truly loving heart is a selfless heart—a disciplined heart.

Jesus, sometimes discipline scares me. It just sounds so hard and unpleasant. Help me to remember that self-discipline is just another name for true love. Help me to love you so much that the little sacrifices required by my fidelity become sweet, like so many chances to show you how much I do love you. Let my discipline never become dry or heartless—keep it full of love.

**Sacred Heart of Jesus, disciplined by love,
make my heart more like yours!**

THURSDAY—WEEK FIVE

Let not your hearts be troubled.

—John 14:1

. . .

At the Last Supper, soon to be taken prisoner and condemned to death, Jesus consoles his disciples as if they were his children. He knows that the next hours will be extremely trying for them. He puts his own fear aside for a moment and seeks to comfort and reassure them. He warns them of what will happen, so that when it comes to pass they will take courage and not lose heart. Here, in this moment of crisis, we find some of the most tender words in the entire gospel.

Jesus doesn't want his own passion to be a stumbling block for his disciples or an obstacle to their faith in God or in him. Jesus' heart was so big that all he could think of in this terrible moment was the good of his friends who had stood by him. He tells them he is going to prepare a place for them in his Father's house. He sets their hearts on heaven, to help them through a terrible ordeal. Even in his darkest hour, he looked to console rather than be consoled. His was truly a reassuring heart, a maternal heart whispering to his children, "Don't worry. Everything will be all right."

Our natural selfishness makes this tough for us. When we are overwhelmed by our own problems and fears, it is tremendously difficult to think of others and their needs. But all of us—men and women alike—are called to develop this maternal dimension of our hearts. We are called to watch over those around us, bolster their confidence, console them, and accompany them through their trials. Sometimes when we feel the weakest, God will give us the grace to be a source of strength for those who are still weaker.

Lord, when I contemplate your example of tenderness and warmth, I am filled with gratitude. Thank you for being there for me in my own life, consoling me in my struggles and emboldening me in my time of doubt. You know my needs better than I do and care for my interests even more than I could. Help me to console and comfort those around me. Let me be a source of encouragement and reassurance to them, paving the way for them to encounter your loving heart through their contact with me.

**Sacred Heart of Jesus, wonderfully reassuring,
make my heart more like yours!**

FRIDAY—WEEK FIVE

Whatever he [the Father] does, that the Son does likewise.
—*John 5:19*

. . .

Some like to think of Jesus as a nonconformist, a revolutionary rebelling against the leaders of his day and forging a new path for religion. But when it came to the Father's will, Jesus wasn't a revolutionary at all. He saved us by his obedience; his Father's will was the guiding light for his decisions.

Obedience has gotten a bad reputation. It can seem subhuman, uncreative, robotic, and downright unpleasant. We prefer, as the bumper sticker says, to "question authority" rather than obey it! But without obedience we'll never understand Jesus' heart. For Jesus, obedience was not inhuman or humiliating. It was, quite simply, an expression of his love for God. More than anything else in the world, he desired to please his Father. His conscience was so clear on this point that he could say, "I always do what is pleasing to him" (John 8:29, *NAB*).

Few of us can say that. Sometimes we don't even ask ourselves whether what we are doing *right now* is pleasing to God or not. Sometimes it's just what we feel like doing. Sometimes it's what we have to do. Sometimes we're not even sure why we're doing what we're doing—but Jesus knew. "I always do what is pleasing to him."

This obedience, this conformity to the Father's will, led to imitation. Jesus was united to the Father in everything and found in the Father not only his source of direction but also his model. Jesus wasn't worried about being innovative or original. "Very truly, I tell you, the Son can do nothing on his own, but only what he sees the Father doing; for whatever the Father does, the Son does likewise" (John 5:19, *NAB*).

When we ask ourselves "What would Jesus do?" we find that he was asking himself the very same question: *What would the Father do?* And that's what he did.

Jesus, I find joy in contemplating your obedient heart. I love to see how much you loved your Father and how you sought to please him in everything. You didn't question. You didn't revolt or dissent. You simply obeyed with full freedom, full consent, and a heart full of love. Teach me to obey like you!

**Sacred Heart of Jesus, obedient to the end,
make my heart more like yours!**

SATURDAY—WEEK FIVE

"Every one is searching for you."... People
came to him from every quarter.

—Mark 1:37, 45

. . .

One of the extraordinary qualities of Jesus' heart is its universality. Quite simply, it seemed to have room for everyone. In Jesus' presence, no one felt excluded, or unimportant, or unwanted. The embrace of Jesus' heart seemed to envelop the entire world. Because of this, he also brought out the best in people. People became less defensive around him and allowed their hearts to open to his.

Not everyone responded this way, of course. There were those who found Jesus threatening, mostly because he upended their way of doing business and challenged them in ways they didn't wish to be challenged. For others, the very openness and universality of Jesus' heart was off-putting, as they espoused a more elitist view of religion and the kingdom of God. They found his mercy particularly distasteful and wondered how he could justify spending so much time with "sinners."

Jesus treated people with the utmost respect. For him there were no social classes or status requirements, no "us" and "them." All people—young and old, men and women, conationals and foreigners—were precious to him. His heart embraced them all. He didn't approve of all sorts of behavior, of course. He clearly distinguished between good and evil. Yet he loved all people, even those who had the misfortune of falling into sin.

This universal heart poses a real challenge to us who follow Jesus. It is terribly hard to love everyone, especially those who appear so downright unlovable. We surround ourselves with people like us, loving them and avoiding the rest. Yet not to love each and every one is to introduce a rift between our hearts and Christ's. Only by loving all, and desiring their eternal salvation, can we attain the union with Christ that we long for.

Lord Jesus, thank you for welcoming everyone. You looked right past appearances and cut to the core of people, finding good in each of them. You saw not only what they were but also what they could be. And this gaze of love and encouragement brought out the best in people. Help me to be this way with the people in my life. Give me eyes to see them the way that you see them, to overlook their faults and disagreeableness in order to find the good and the beautiful. My heart should exclude no one, just as yours didn't.

Sacred Heart of Jesus, universal in your love for all, make my heart more like yours!

Holy Week

Jesus spoke of longing for his "hour" to arrive, and finally it is here. It is true that Jesus came to preach, teach, and heal, yet above all he came to save us through his passion and death. He came to show us the depths of his love, since no one has a greater love than the one who lays down his life for his friends. And now that critical moment has arrived. It is time for us to intensify our union with Jesus and above all to commit ourselves to remain by his side, accompanying him in his hour of need.

Lord Jesus, I love you with all my heart. Thank you for these beautiful weeks we have spent together and for revealing your Sacred Heart to me. The more I get to know you, the deeper my love for you becomes and the more I yearn to be like you. We are beginning the toughest week of your life, a week when your closest friends abandoned you and you were left all alone. Please give me the strength to stay by your side, awake with you. I beg you to find some consolation in my heart, as I have found in yours. This would be my greatest pleasure and privilege. Amen.

PALM SUNDAY

Fear not, daughter of Zion; behold, your king
is coming, sitting on a donkey's colt!
—*John 12:15*

. . .

On Palm Sunday, the disciples rejoice. The hour of his—and their—triumph has finally arrived. Finally, the people have risen up and recognized Jesus as the Messiah, the Son of David. The crowds come out in droves to gaze on him, singing his praises and laying their cloaks as well as palm and olive branches in his path. His enemies despair, aware that now the whole world is running after him and there is nothing more to be done.

Only Jesus knows the truth. He accepts their accolades and grimly smiles as he makes his way toward his death. Earlier, when the crowds tried to carry him off to proclaim him king, he quietly slipped through their midst and made his way off to pray. His kingdom is not of this world. But now Jesus docilely accepts the momentary celebration, knowing full well that these same fickle masses will be screaming for his crucifixion five days later.

Jesus knows that fame and celebrity mean nothing. They come and go at a moment's notice and do not reflect who we are. We are no better when people love and praise us, and no worse because they revile us. Jesus walks toward the cross out of love for us and because it is his Father's will. We too are called to imitate this same detachment that we see in Christ, looking for approval from God alone. True success is measured not by ratings but by our faithfulness to God.

Jesus, what a beautiful example of serenity you give us in the face of your passion! You know how the opinion of the crowds can change from one day to the next, and instead you look to the Father for guidance. As you enter Jerusalem, you walk not toward earthly glory but toward the supreme example of love for God and humanity—the giving of your life for us. Help me, dear Jesus, to face my crosses with the same peace of soul and the same devotion to God and his holy will.

**Sacred Heart of Jesus, serene before the cross,
make my heart more like yours!**

MONDAY—HOLY WEEK

Love is patient.

—1 Corinthians 13:4

. . .

· ·

More than once, Jesus manifested exasperation because those who approached him lacked faith. Jesus worked so many signs and wonders, but for some it was never enough. Through it all, though, he revealed a remarkably patient heart. He put up with a lot!

In his celebrated list of the qualities of Christian love, St. Paul places patience in first place (cf. 1 Corinthians 13:4–5). Patience (from the Latin *patiens*) is our ability to suffer. This is a perfect description of Christ's own heart. He was truly patient, suffering through things that few of us would have the forbearance to endure: the slowness of others to understand, their resistance to God's grace, their lessons unlearned, worldly standards, pettiness, jealousy, and betrayal.

After the resurrection, the examples of this patience continue. The two disciples of Emmaus abandon all hope after the death of Jesus and decide to return to their homes (cf. Luke 24:13–35). Ever the Good Shepherd, Jesus doesn't simply let them leave but rather meets them on the road, patiently explaining to them the prophecies in Scripture. His gentle reproach, "How foolish you are, and how slow to believe all that the prophets have declared!" (Luke 24:25, *NAB*), is clothed in mildness and love.

Each of us has experienced the patient love of Christ firsthand. How many times we have failed him in matters little and great, yet he doesn't give up on us. How long he has waited for us to respond to his grace, and yet he has waited! Jesus' patience is a marvelous lesson for us Christians, who can get so frustrated with others' failings and our own slow progress. When others seem to slow us down, when people don't "get it," when we feel let down by someone we counted on, we must remember the way Christ treated his disciples and the way he has dealt with us. We all must bear one another's crosses at times, knowing that others have often borne ours.

Jesus, how great is your patience! You surrounded yourself with common men and women, bearing with their defects, limitations, and human failings. I too am frail and full of flaws. I have failed you many times, yet you never give up on me. Thank you for being so patient with me—let me be worthy of your patience and patient with others in return!

Sacred Heart of Jesus, ever patient,
make my heart more like yours!

TUESDAY—HOLY WEEK

Peace I leave with you; my peace I give to you.
Not as the world gives do I give it to you. Do
not let your hearts be troubled or afraid.

—*John 14:27,* NAB

. . .

At the Last Supper, Jesus offers his disciples a share in his own peace, a different sort than the world gives. He removes our fears and fills us with his Holy Spirit. Peace is both a choice and a gift. It is a choice, as love and trust in God bring peace to the heart. It is a gift, as Jesus offers us a sharing in his own perfect peace.

Jesus truly had a peaceful heart. He was at peace with the Father, with humanity, and with all creation. A soul at prayer is a soul at peace, and Jesus lived in constant contact with his Father. His trust was absolute, as was his loving, filial acceptance of the Father's will. The deepest sources of peace—trust, single-heartedness, generosity, openness to God's will—all characterized the heart of Christ. He feared nothing, since he had the Father's love, which meant he had everything.

Jesus became our peace; on the cross he healed man's enmity with God. The peace that matters most is the peace that Jesus won for us: peace with God. This is the beginning of any lasting peace between peoples. The true peace he promises is not a superficial "getting along" with everybody but the deeper peace that comes from communion with God.

As Christians seeking a heart like Christ's, we are called to live in peace and to be builders of peace. By working for justice, by growing in trust in God, by casting out fear and anxiety, by detaching ourselves from aspirations that clash with the Father's will, by building bridges between people, by forgiving offenses, we become instruments and channels of Christ's peace, a peace that the world cannot produce.

Prince of Peace, grant me a peaceful heart. Your will is my peace. In loving submission to your plan for my life, I find peace and fulfillment. So often I am the cause of my own anxiety and unrest. Teach me to let go of everything outside of your will for me.

**Sacred Heart of Jesus, filled with peace,
make my heart more like yours!**

WEDNESDAY—HOLY WEEK

My soul is sorrowful even to death. Remain
here and keep watch with me.
—*Matthew 26:38,* NAB

. . .

When Peter's mother-in law was sick, Jesus was there to cure her. When the centurion's servant was at death's door, Jesus was there to heal him. When the disciples foundered in the stormy sea, Jesus was there to calm the tempest. When the holy women wept in sorrow, Jesus was there to console them. All through the gospel we find a constant: Jesus is there for people. He meets their needs. He comes to them in times of distress and accompanies them.

And yet a strange thing happens during Holy Week. In the Garden of Gethsemane the tables are turned and it is Jesus who begs to be accompanied. It is Jesus who, in his grief and distress, asks *us* to stay with *him.* Usually so in control, Jesus is overcome by loneliness and sorrow and turns to his disciples for comfort.

Jesus doesn't ask the disciples to fight for him. He doesn't request help to escape the Passion he is to undergo. He simply asks them to be with him, by his side, in his hour of need. In similar fashion, Jesus doesn't appeal to us to resolve the world's problems or to undertake tremendous exploits to show our love for him. He asks us to stay close, to pray with him, to stand awake by his side. He who is *always* there for us requests that this week we be by him. He requests nothing more than our silence, our company, and our love.

Lord Jesus, you are the truly faithful friend, always present in our time of need. Thank you for choosing to need me as well. Thank you for giving me the incredible honor of consoling you with my presence this week. I gratefully accept your invitation to stay close by you, to pray with you, and to comfort you in your hour of need.

Sacred Heart of Jesus, faithful companion of those in sorrow, make my heart more like yours!

HOLY THURSDAY—HOLY WEEK

This is my body which is given for you.

—*Luke 22:19*

. . .

• •

The essence of love is self-donation. Jesus says that the greatest love a person can have is to "lay down his life for his friends." This laying down of one's life can be literal or figurative, but in Jesus' case it was absolutely literal.

On the night before he suffered, Jesus was at supper with his disciples. He took bread, said the blessing, broke the bread, and gave it to them, saying, "This is my body, which is given for you" (Luke 22:19, NAB). He took his life in his hands and delivered it over to his apostles. He became their food, their sustenance, their Eucharist. Prefiguring the death he would suffer the following day, Jesus offered his body and blood in sacrifice to God and also as the bread of angels.

What was Jesus thinking as he held up that bread and distributed it to those around him? What was going on in his heart? What memories came rushing through his mind? What hopes and desires? It was most certainly an act of love. He was giving himself as totally and perfectly as a human being can. He wanted to be there for his disciples—for all of us—in this moment and throughout the centuries. He wanted to be our comfort, our strength, our consolation, our home.

This act was the culmination of a life of self-offering that began with the Incarnation. The whole reason for his coming into the world was to offer himself up. Jesus had a eucharistic heart, a heart offered up continually to the Father and those around him. Jesus accepted fatigue, hardships, travels, misunderstandings, and betrayals—anything as long as it could be of service for us, his friends. Whatever the cost, Jesus didn't hold back.

The Eucharist is service. It is humility. It is sacrifice. It is self-gift. If we are attentive, we will find that we have numerous opportunities to be eucharistic with one another, to participate in Jesus' eucharistic heart.

Lord Jesus, make me a gift for my brothers and sisters. Let me serve them truly, anticipating their needs and giving myself without reserve. It is an honor to do so in your name. In serving them, grant me a share in your heart, your sentiments, your dispositions.

Sacred Heart of Jesus, sharing your body and blood, make my heart more like yours!

GOOD FRIDAY—HOLY WEEK

Father, into your hands I commit my spirit!

—*Luke 23:46*

. . .

• •

It would be the perfect scene for an action movie. The captured hero patiently awaits the moment to turn on his assailants, ready to slay them in just retribution for their crimes. They think they have him trapped, and yet at the perfect moment he escapes from their clutches and reveals his power. The good guys cry out in jubilation for the triumph of good over evil.

And yet that's not how the scene plays out, is it? Jesus' enemies taunt him, promising that if he'll but come down from the cross, they'll believe in him (cf. Matthew 27:40–43). All Jesus has to do is demonstrate his power and the whole world would follow him. But that is not the sort of messiah Jesus is. He came to show the depths of his love. Obedient to the Father's will, he came to die for us. He came to embrace "failure" and rejection, out of love for us. His victory over sin and death is of a different sort, a higher sort. Like a gentle lamb he goes to the slaughter and opens not his mouth. He, the Lamb of God, takes on himself the sins of the world and dies in our stead. The sins he bears are yours and mine, as is the punishment he takes for us.

If we are to be disciples of Jesus, we must accept his way. He does not promise earthly success. He does not promise that people will love us. He does not promise glory as the world understands it. He promises persecution and the opportunity to give our lives for the salvation of the world. On Good Friday we celebrate the victory of love over hatred, of life over death, of good over evil. But victory comes through the cross. *Per crucem ad lucem.*

Lord Jesus, like St. Peter we think there must be another way, a better way. We do not want to embrace the cross as our path to salvation. Yet you show us that the path of true love is a path of total self-giving and surrender. Teach me to follow your example. Let me always look to you as my model and my Lord.

**Sacred Heart of Jesus, crucified out of love for me,
make my heart more like yours!**

HOLY SATURDAY

Behold, your mother!

—John 19:27

. . .

When I meet someone's parents for the first time, I am almost always struck by the resemblances. Sometimes they're physical, but still more often they're found in recognizable gestures—a tilt of the head, a characteristic motion of the hands. Without realizing it, we assimilate an awful lot from the people we spend the most time with. After spending thirty years living with Mary, Jesus surely resembled her in numerous ways. The disciples would have picked this up at once, and after Jesus' resurrection her presence in their midst was a constant reminder to them of her son.

But of the ways Mary was like Jesus, surely the most characteristic of all was in the heart. Jesus was her beloved son, and he was also her God. She learned from him even as he learned from her. Luke's Gospel describes Mary as profoundly contemplative and spiritual, saying she "kept all these [words], pondering them in her heart" (Luke 2:19). She stored away the marvelous memories of God's action in her life, turning them over and over.

Like Jesus, Mary had a prayerful heart, a contemplative heart. She was not impetuous or superficial but thoughtful and profound. Like Jesus, Mary's heart was pure, undivided, compassionate, merciful, patient, courageous—full of the many virtues we've considered in this lenten volume. She was obedient as he was, asking only that it "be done to me according to your word," or, as Jesus always prayed, "not my will but yours be done."

Today, Holy Saturday, we meditate on Mary's immaculate heart, a sorrowful heart grieving the death of her son—a hopeful heart, holding on to belief in his resurrection. We contemplate her as the Mother of Sorrows sharing in his Passion, knowing that mother and son can never be far apart. We can always trust that Mary's heart will lead us ever closer to the Sacred Heart of Jesus.

Lord Jesus, we all need intercessors, and we all need models of what it means to follow you. Thank you for the treasure of your saints and especially for the Queen of Heaven, your mother Mary. Because she humbled herself as the "handmaid of the Lord," you exalted her. Let me imitate her heart so that I too may become more like you.

**Marian heart of Jesus,
make my heart more like yours!**

Easter Sunday

Peace be with you. As the Father has
sent me, even so I send you.

—*John 20:21*

. . .

Easter is God's confirmation of the "acceptable sacrifice" of Jesus. His surrender to death defeated death, robbing it of its power over humanity. Death no longer had a hold on Jesus or on those who participate in the grace of his sacrifice. Easter is the victory of life and love. The grain of wheat that fell to the earth has borne the abundant fruit of salvation from sin.

Yet Easter doesn't stop there. When Jesus appears to his disciples that first Easter Sunday, he greets them and immediately confirms their participation in his mission. "As the Father has sent me," he tells them, "so I am sending you." Jesus is the first "apostle" (one who is sent), whom the Father has dispatched from Heaven to be our Savior. That same mission Jesus entrusts to his followers—to each of us—making us sharers in his project of salvation for all mankind. On the cross Jesus had given his report to the Father: *Consummatum est*—Mission accomplished!

By baptism every Christian is "sent" on mission. Every Christian is an apostle, sent out by Jesus to bear witness to the world, witness of the Good News of salvation in Christ. Christians are by nature active rather than passive, not only recipients of the gift of salvation but also workers in the vineyard of the Lord. And there is much work to be done. During his public ministry Jesus looked at the crowds and saw them as sheep without a shepherd, as an abundant harvest in need of reaping. And he exclaimed, "The harvest is plentiful, but the laborers are few; pray therefore the Lord of the harvest to send out laborers into his harvest"

(Matthew 9:37). Each of us is sent out from his or her own place to work, to witness, and to announce the gospel to all of creation. The world hungers and thirsts for Jesus, and many wait for us to make him known. If we don't do it, who will?

Lord Jesus, thank you for deigning to share your life and mission with us! Thank you for the grace of participating with you in the work of salvation. What a privilege to bear your message of grace and mercy to those around us! Make me a faithful apostle of your love. Send your Holy Spirit upon your missionary Church so that we may worthily proclaim you to the entire world.

Apostolic Heart of Jesus, faithful to your mission until the end, make my heart more like yours!

TRADITIONAL PRAYERS TO THE SACRED HEART OF JESUS

Morning Offering to the Sacred Heart

O Jesus! Through the Immaculate Heart of Mary, I offer you my prayers, works, joys, and sufferings of this day for all the intentions of your Sacred Heart, in union with the holy sacrifice of the Mass throughout the world, in reparation for my sins, for the intentions of all our associates, and in particular for the intentions of the Holy Father. Amen.

—Apostleship of Prayer

Morning Offering

O my God! I offer Thee all the actions of this day for the intentions and for the glory of the Sacred Heart of Jesus. I desire to sanctify every beat of my heart, my every thought, my simplest works, by uniting them to Its infinite merits; and I wish to make reparation for my sins by casting them into the furnace of Its merciful love.

—St. Teresa of the Child Jesus

Novena of Confidence

Lord Jesus! To your Sacred Heart I entrust this intention. [Here mention your request.]
Only look upon me,
Then do what your Heart inspires.
Let your Heart decide.
I count on it.

I trust in it.
I throw myself on Its mercy.
Lord Jesus! You will not fail me.

******

Sacred Heart of Jesus! Protect our families.

Invocation to the Sacred Heart of Jesus

To your adoration and your burning love, I unite myself.
To your ardent zeal and your reparations, I unite myself.
To your thanksgiving and your firm confidence, I unite myself.
To your humility and your obedience, I unite myself.
To your gentleness and your peace, I unite myself
To your surpassing kindness and your universal charity, I unite myself.
To your intense desire for the conversion of sinners, I unite myself.
To your close union with your heavenly Father, I unite myself.
To your intentions, desires, and will, I unite myself.

Love of the Heart of Jesus, inflame my heart.
Strength of the Heart of Jesus, uphold my heart.
Mercy of the Heart of Jesus, forgive my heart.
Patience of the Heart of Jesus, do not weary of my heart.
Kingdom of the Heart of Jesus, be established in my heart.
Wisdom of the Heart of Jesus, teach my heart.
Will of the Heart of Jesus, dispose of my heart.
Zeal of the Heart of Jesus, consume my heart.

Prayer for Peace of Heart

O most Sacred, most loving Heart of Jesus!
Thou art concealed in the Holy Eucharist,

And thou beatest for us still.
Now, as then, thou sayest:
"With desire I have desired."
I worship thee, then,
With all my best love and awe,
With fervent affection,
With my most subdued, most resolved will....
When Thou for a while take up thy abode within me,
O make my heart beat with thy Heart!
Purify it of all that is earthly,
All that is proud and sensual,
All that is hard and cruel,
Of all perversity,
Of all disorder,
Of all deadness.
So fill it with Thee,
That neither the events of the day
Nor the circumstances of the time
May have the power to ruffle it,
But that in thy love and thy fear
It may have peace.
—John Henry Cardinal Newman

******

Sweet Heart of my Jesus! Grant that I may ever love thee more.

******

Sacred Heart of Jesus! I give myself to thee through Mary.

Act of Reparation to the Sacred Heart

Most sweet Jesus, whose overflowing charity for men is requited by so much forgetfulness, negligence, and contempt, behold us prostrate before you, eager to repair by a special act of homage the cruel indifference and injuries to which your loving Heart is everywhere subject.

Mindful, alas! that we ourselves have had a share in such great indignities, which we now deplore from the depths of our hearts, we humbly ask your pardon and declare our readiness to atone by voluntary expiation not only for our own personal offenses but also for the sins of those who, straying far from the path of salvation, refuse in their obstinate infidelity to follow you, their Shepherd and Leader, or, renouncing the promises of their baptism, have cast off the sweet yoke of your law.

We are now resolved to expiate each and every deplorable outrage committed against you; we are now determined to make amends for the manifold offenses against Christian modesty in unbecoming dress and behavior, for all the foul seductions laid to ensnare the feet of the innocent, for the frequent violations of Sundays and holy days, and for the shocking blasphemies uttered against you and your saints. We wish also to make amends for the insults to which your Vicar on earth and your priests are subjected; for the profanation, by conscious neglect or terrible acts of sacrilege, of the very Sacrament of your Divine Love; and lastly for the public crimes of nations who resist the rights and teaching authority of the Church which you have founded.

Would that we were able to wash away such abominations with our blood. We now offer, in reparation for these violations of your divine honor, the satisfaction you once made to your Eternal Father on the cross and that you continue to renew daily on our altars; we offer it in union with the acts of atonement of your Virgin Mother and all the saints and of the pious faithful on earth; and we sincerely promise to make recompense, as far as we can with the help of thy grace, for all neglect of your great love and for the sins we and others have committed in the past. Henceforth, we will live a life of unswerving faith, of purity of conduct, of perfect observance of the precepts of the gospel and especially that of charity. We promise to the best of our power to prevent others from offending you and to bring as many as possible to follow you.

O loving Jesus, through the intercession of the Blessed Virgin Mother, our model in reparation, deign to receive the voluntary offering we make of this act of expiation; and by the crowning gift of perseverance keep us faithful unto death in our duty and the allegiance we owe you, so that we may all one day come to that happy home, where with the Father and the Holy Spirit you live and reign, God, forever and ever. Amen.

Litany of the Most Sacred Heart of Jesus
V/ Lord, have mercy.
R/ Lord, have mercy.

V/ Christ, have mercy.
R/ Christ, have mercy.

V/ Lord, have mercy.
R/ Lord, have mercy.

V/ Jesus, hear us.
R/ Jesus, graciously hear us.

V/ God, the Father of Heaven,
R/ Have mercy on us.
God the Son, Redeemer of the world, / Have mercy on us.
God the Holy Spirit, / Have mercy on us.
Holy Trinity, One God, / Have mercy on us.
Heart of Jesus, Son of the Eternal Father, / Have mercy on us.
Heart of Jesus, formed by the Holy Spirit in the womb of the Virgin

Mother, / Have mercy on us.

Heart of Jesus, substantially united to the Word of God, / Have mercy on us.

Heart of Jesus, of Infinite Majesty, / Have mercy on us.

Heart of Jesus, Sacred Temple of God, / Have mercy on us.

Heart of Jesus, Tabernacle of the Most High, / Have mercy on us.

Heart of Jesus, House of God and Gate of Heaven, / Have mercy on us.

Heart of Jesus, burning furnace of charity, / Have mercy on us.

Heart of Jesus, abode of justice and love, / Have mercy on us.

Heart of Jesus, full of goodness and love, / Have mercy on us.

Heart of Jesus, abyss of all virtues, / Have mercy on us.

Heart of Jesus, most worthy of all praise, / Have mercy on us.

Heart of Jesus, king and center of all hearts, / Have mercy on us.

Heart of Jesus, in whom are all the treasures of wisdom and knowledge, / Have mercy on us.

Heart of Jesus, in whom the Father was well pleased, / Have mercy on us.

Heart of Jesus, of whose fullness we have all received, / Have mercy on us.

Heart of Jesus, desire of the everlasting hills, / Have mercy on us.

Heart of Jesus, patient and most merciful, / Have mercy on us.

Heart of Jesus, enriching all who invoke you, / Have mercy on us.

Heart of Jesus, fountain of life and holiness, / Have mercy on us.

Heart of Jesus, propitiation for our sins, / Have mercy on us.

Heart of Jesus, loaded down with opprobrium, / Have mercy on us.

Heart of Jesus, bruised for our offenses, / Have mercy on us.

Heart of Jesus, obedient unto death, / Have mercy on us.

Heart of Jesus, pierced with a lance, / Have mercy on us.

Heart of Jesus, source of all consolation, / Have mercy on us.

Heart of Jesus, our life and resurrection, / Have mercy on us.

Heart of Jesus, our peace and reconciliation, / Have mercy on us.

Heart of Jesus, victim for our sins, / Have mercy on us.

Heart of Jesus, salvation of those who trust in you, / Have mercy on us.

Heart of Jesus, hope of those who die in you, / Have mercy on us.

Heart of Jesus, delight of all the saints, / Have mercy on us.

V/ Lamb of God, who take away the sins of the world,

R/ Spare us, O Lord.

V/ Lamb of God, who take away the sins of the world,

R/ Graciously hear us, O Lord.

V/ Lamb of God, who take away the sins of the world,

R/ Have mercy on us.

V/ Jesus, meek and humble of heart,

R/ Make our hearts like yours.

Let us pray. Almighty and eternal God, look upon the Heart of your most beloved Son and upon the praises and satisfaction that he offers you in the name of sinners; and to those who implore your mercy, in your great goodness, grant forgiveness in the name of the same Jesus Christ, your Son, who lives and reigns with you forever and ever.

R/ Amen.

Prayer for Perseverance

O adorable Heart of my Jesus, Heart created by God's love for men! Until now I have shown toward you only ingratitude. Pardon me, O Heart of my Jesus, abyss of love and of mercy. How is it possible that I do not die of sorrow when I reflect on your goodness to me and my ingratitude to you? You, my Creator, after having created me, have given your blood and your life for me. Not content with this, you have invented a means of offering thyself up every day for me in the Holy Eucharist, exposing thyself to a thousand insults and outrages. Ah, Jesus, do wound my heart with great contrition for my sins and lively love for you. Through your tears and your blood give me the grace of perseverance in your fervent love until I breathe my last sigh. Amen.

—*St. Alphonsus de Liguori*

Contemporary Prayer of Reparation

Lord Jesus, who loves us so much: We have not loved you as we easily might have, nor served You enough in our neighbor as we could have. We are truly sorry for this unfaithful love and promise to do better in the future. Because you accept everything that we do in God's grace when done in a spirit of love and obedience, for reparation we now offer you and your Heart our every thought, word, deed, and suffering in union with your own sufferings. Join our reparation to that which you ceaselessly offer to the Father in the Mass and in the silence of the tabernacle. Help us to suffer lovingly and to aid those who suffer. Make your redemptive love fruitful in the hearts of all those who will die today, so that all of us may love you for ever in heaven. Amen.

—*www.sacredheartdevotion.com*

Prayer for Health

O Sacred Heart of Jesus, I come to ask of your infinite mercy the gift of health and strength that I may serve you more faithfully and love you more sincerely than in the past. I wish to be well and strong if this be your good pleasure and for your greater glory. Filled with high resolve and determined to perform my tasks most perfectly for love of you, I wish to be enabled to go back to my duties. Amen.

—*www.prayerbook.com*

Prayer to the Sacred Heart for Priests

Remember, O most loving Heart of Jesus, that they for whom I pray are those for whom you prayed so earnestly the night before your death. These are they to whom you look to continue with you in your sorrows when others forsake you, who share your griefs and have inherited your persecutions, according to your word: That the servant is not greater than his Lord. Remember, O Heart of Jesus, that they are the objects of the world's hatred and Satan's deadliest snares. Keep them then, O Jesus, in the safe citadel of your Sacred Heart and there let them be sanctified in truth. May they be one with you and one among themselves, and grant that multitudes may be brought through their word to believe in you and love you.

Prayer for Someone Special

May the grace of the Sacred Heart be with you,
The peace of the Sacred Heart encompass you;
The merits of the Sacred Heart plead for you;
The love of the Sacred Heart inflame you;
The sorrows of the Sacred Heart console you;
The zeal of the Sacred Heart animate you;
The virtues of the Sacred Heart shine forth in your word and work;
And may the joys of the beatific vision be your eternal reward. Amen.

—www.prayerbook.com

Plea to Jesus

Jesus of the Eucharist! Come to us and be our Ruler. All that we have and are is thine to command, for all that we have is thine. If our hearts are poor, enrich them with thy Grace. If they have been wretched and stained, accept them purged and cleansed through the Immaculate Heart of Mary.

SUFFERING HEART of Jesus! To thee we confide all the trials of our souls.

SWEET HEART of Jesus! To thy care we confide our weaknesses, and we ask thee to accept our sincere repentance.

COMPASSIONATE HEART of Jesus! We confide our souls to thee, tormented by our suffering conscience.

GENTLE HEART of Jesus! We confide to thee the peace and salvation of our families.

EUCHARISTIC HEART of Jesus! The world, worried unto death, finds a refuge in thy Heart, where the lance once opened for us the source of Life.

Come, O Jesus! Be our Brother in the pure joy of Christian love!

Come, O Jesus! Be our Friend in the depths of this world's sorrows. Amen.

—www.prayerbook.com

Prayer to the Eternal Father

O eternal Father, through the divine Heart of Jesus, I adore you for all those who adore you not; I love you for all those who do not love you. I go in spirit through the whole world to seek for souls redeemed by the blood of Jesus. I embrace them in order to present them to you in his Sacred Heart, and in union with your merciful Heart, I ask for their conversion.

—Blessed Marie of the Incarnation

******

Jesus is the only true friend of our hearts.

—St. Margaret Mary Alacoque

Prayer Before an Image or Picture of the Sacred Heart

O Sacred Heart of Jesus, pour out your benedictions upon the Holy Church, upon its priests, and upon all its children. Sustain the just, convert the sinners, assist the dying, deliver the souls in purgatory, and extend over all hearts the sweet empire of your love. Amen.

O Lord Jesus Christ, whose whole life was one continual sacrifice for the glory of your Father and the salvation of our souls, grant us the grace to find our joy in making sacrifices for you and for the interests of your Sacred Heart. Amen.

A Salutation Prayer

Hail, Heart of Jesus, save me!

Hail, Heart of my Creator, perfect me!

Hail, Heart of my Savior, deliver me!

Hail, Heart of my Judge, grant me pardon!

Hail, Heart of my Father, govern me!

Hail, Heart of my Spouse, grant me love!

Hail, Heart of my Master, teach me!

Hail, Heart of my King, be my crown!

Hail, Heart of my Benefactor, enrich me!

Hail, Heart of my Shepherd, guard me!

Hail, Heart of my Friend, comfort me!

Hail, Heart of my Brother, stay with me!

Hail, Heart of the Child Jesus, draw me to thyself!

Hail, Heart of Jesus dying on the Cross, redeem me!

Hail, Heart of Jesus in all Thy states, give thyself to me!

Hail, Heart of incomparable goodness, have mercy on me!

Hail, Heart of splendor, shine within me!

Hail, most loving Heart, inflame me!

Hail, most merciful Heart, work within me!

Hail, most humble Heart, dwell within me!

Hail, most patient Heart, support me!

Hail, most faithful Heart, be my reward!

Hail, most admirable and most worthy Heart, bless me!

—St. Margaret Mary Alacoque

Act of Consecration

I, (your name), give myself and consecrate to the Sacred Heart of our Lord Jesus Christ my person and my life, my actions, pains, and sufferings, so that I may be unwilling to make use of any part of my being save to honor, love, and glorify the Sacred Heart.

This is my unchanging purpose, namely, to be all his, and to do all things for the love of him, at the same time renouncing with all my heart whatever is displeasing to him.

I therefore take You, O Sacred Heart, to be the only object of my love, the guardian of my life, my assurance of salvation, the remedy of my weakness and inconstancy, the atonement for all the faults of my life and my sure refuge at the hour of death.

Be then, O Heart of goodness, my justification before God your Father, and turn away from me the strokes of his righteous anger. O Heart of love, I put all my confidence in you, for I fear everything from my own wickedness and frailty; but I hope for all things from your goodness and bounty.

Do consume in me all that can displease you or resist your holy will. Let your pure love imprint you so deeply upon my heart that I shall nevermore be able to forget you or to be separated from you. May I obtain from all your loving-kindness the grace of having my name written in you, for in you I desire to place all my happiness and all my glory, living and dying in true bondage to you.

—*St. Margaret Mary Alacoque*

Devotion to the Sacred Heart of Jesus

Devotion to the Sacred Heart grew especially out of a series of visions experienced by Margaret Mary of Alacoque (1647–1690), a Visitation sister at the monastery of Paray-le-Monial in France. Obviously, devotion to Jesus' love for man did not begin there. St. John speaks of God so loving the world as to give his only son to be its savior (cf. John 3:16). St. Paul wrote: "I live by faith in the Son of God, who loved me and gave himself for me" (Galatians 2:20). Devotion to the wounds of Christ focused especially on the wound from the soldier's lance in his side, and the blood and water that flowed from his open heart were seen by the Fathers of the Church as representing all the sacramental graces flowing to the Church from Jesus' heart.

Some saints of the Middle Ages, such as St. Mechtilde (d. 1298) and St. Gertrude (d. 1302), were especially dedicated to the heart of Christ, and it slowly grew into a fairly common "private devotion" especially by the sixteenth century. It was St. John Eudes (1602–1680) who made the devotion "public," honoring it with an office and establishing a feast for it. But it was above all through Margaret Mary that this devotion was established and propagated throughout the universal Church.

Margaret Mary received numerous revelations. In 1673, on the feast of St. John the Evangelist, Jesus permitted Margaret Mary to rest her head on his heart and then revealed to her the wonders of his love, telling her that he desired to make them known to all mankind. He had chosen her for this work.

Jesus requested to be honored under the symbol of his heart of flesh and asked for a devotion of atoning love, with special emphasis on frequent reception of Holy Communion, Communion on the First Friday of each month, and the observance of the Holy Hour on Thursday evenings, in remembrance of the agony in the Garden of Gethsemane.

During the octave of Corpus Christi, 1675, Margaret Mary received her "great apparition," when Jesus said to her: "Behold the Heart that has so loved men.... Instead of gratitude I receive from the greater part [of mankind] only ingratitude." At this time Jesus asked her for a feast of reparation to be celebrated on the Friday after the octave of Corpus Christi and told her to consult with her spiritual director, the Jesuit priest Fr. Claude de la Colombière (now a saint himself). Fr. de la Colombière believed in the authenticity of Margaret Mary's revelations and advised her to write an account of the apparition. For his part, Fr. de la Colombière became a zealous apostle of this devotion, consecrating himself to the Sacred Heart and propagating it wherever he could.

It wasn't until 1856, however, that the feast of the Sacred Heart of Jesus was extended to the universal Church by Pope Pius IX. Some forty years later, on June 11, 1899, Pope Leo XIII solemnly consecrated the entire world to the Sacred Heart; Leo would refer to it as the "great act" of his pontificate. He declared devotion to the Sacred Heart to be "the most acceptable form of piety" and said it would be "profitable to all."

Important Papal Encyclicals on Devotion to the Sacred Heart of Jesus
Leo XIII, encyclical letter *Annum Sacrum*, May 25, 1899.
Pius XI, encyclical letter *Miserentissimus Redemptor*, May 8, 1928.
Pius XI, encyclical letter *Caritate Christi Compulsi*, May 3, 1932.
Pius XII, encyclical letter *Haurietis Aquas*, May 15, 1956.

St. Margaret Mary Alacoque

Margaret Mary was chosen by Christ to arouse the Church to a realization of the love of God symbolized by the Heart of Jesus.

Her early years were marked by sickness and a painful home situation. "The heaviest of my crosses," she once said, "was that I could do nothing to lighten the cross my mother was suffering." After considering marriage for some time, Margaret entered the Order of Visitation nuns at the age of twenty-four.

A Visitation sister was "not to be extraordinary except by being ordinary," but the young nun was not to enjoy this anonymity. A fellow novice (the shrewdest of critics) termed Margaret humble, simple, and frank but above all kind and patient under sharp criticism and correction. She could not meditate in the formal way expected, though she tried her best to give up her "prayer of simplicity." Slow, quiet, and clumsy, she was assigned to help an infirmarian who was a bundle of energy.

On December 21, 1674, three years a nun, she received the first of her revelations. She felt "invested" with the presence of God, though always afraid of deceiving herself in such matters. The request of Christ was that his love for humankind be made evident through her. During the next thirteen months he appeared to her at intervals. His human heart was to be the symbol of his divine-human love. By her own love she was to make up for the coldness and ingratitude of the world—by frequent and loving Holy Communion, especially on the first Friday of each month, and by an hour's vigil of prayer every Thursday night in memory of his agony and isolation in Gethsemane. He also asked that a feast of reparation be instituted.

Like all saints, Margaret had to pay for her gift of holiness. Some of her own sisters were hostile. Theologians who were called in declared her visions delusions and suggested that she eat more heartily. Later, parents of children she taught called her an impostor, an unorthodox innovator. Fr. Claude de la Colombière, a new confessor, recognized her genuineness and supported her. Against her great resistance, Christ called her to be a sacrificial victim for the shortcomings of her own sisters and to make this known.

After serving as novice mistress and assistant superior, she died at the age of forty-three while being anointed, saying, "I need nothing but God, and to lose myself in the heart of Jesus."

St. Margaret Mary was canonized by Pope Benedict XV in 1920.
—*Adapted from "St. Margaret Mary Alacoque,"*
Saint of the Day, *AmericanCatholic.org*

Promises of the Sacred Heart of Jesus
1. I will give them all the graces necessary in their state of life.
2. I will establish peace in their homes.
3. I will comfort them in all their afflictions.
4. I will be their secure refuge during life and above all in death.
5. I will bestow a large blessing upon all their undertakings.
6. Sinners shall find in My Heart the source and the infinite ocean of mercy.
7. Tepid souls shall grow fervent.
8. Fervent souls shall quickly mount to high perfection.
9. I will bless every place where a picture of My Heart shall be set up and honored.
10. I will give to priests the gift of touching the most hardened hearts.

11. Those who shall promote this devotion shall have their names written in My Heart, never to be blotted out.

12. I promise you in the excessive mercy of my Heart that my all-powerful love will grant to all those who communicate on the first Friday in nine consecutive months the grace of final perseverance; they shall not die in my disgrace nor without receiving their sacraments; my divine Heart shall be their safe refuge in this last moment.